MILITARY  PSYCHOLOGY

Volume 15, Number 3, 2003

Special Issue:
Organizational Commitment in the Military
Guest Editor:
Paul A. Gade

JOURNAL INFORMATION

Subscriptions: *Military Psychology* is published quarterly by Lawrence Erlbaum Associates, Inc., 10 Industrial Avenue, Mahwah, NJ 07430–2262. Subscriptions for Volume 15, 2003 are available only on a calendar-year basis.

Subscriptions to *Military Psychology* are provided automatically to members of Division 19, American Psychological Association, paid out of their dues.

Individual rates: **Print *Plus* Online:** $60.00 in USA, $90.00 outside USA. Institutional rates: **Print-Only:** $355.00 in USA, $385.00 outside USA. **Online-Only:** $355.00 in USA and outside USA. **Print *Plus* Online:** $395.00 in USA, $425.00 outside USA. Visit LEA's Web site at http://www.erlbaum.com to view a free sample.

Order subscriptions through the Journal Subscription Department, Lawrence Erlbaum Associates, Inc., 10 Industrial Avenue, Mahwah, NJ 07430–2262.

Claims: Claims for missing copies cannot be honored beyond 4 months after mailing date. Duplicate copies cannot be sent to replace issues not delivered due to failure to notify publisher of change of address.

Change of Address: If you are NOT a member of APA, Division 19, please send address changes to the Journal Subscription Department, Lawrence Erlbaum Associates, Inc., 10 Industrial Avenue, Mahwah, NJ 07430–2262. Division 19 members should contact Keith Cooke, Division 19 Administrative Office, American Psychological Association, 750 First Street NE, Washington, DC 20002–4242.

Permissions: Special requests for permission should be sent to the Permissions Department, Lawrence Erlbaum Associates, Inc., 10 Industrial Avenue, Mahwah, NJ 07430–2262.

Abstracts/Indexes: This journal is abstracted or indexed in *PsycINFO/Psychological Abstracts; Cambridge Scientific Abstracts: Health & Safety Science Abstracts, Risk Abstracts; Ergonomics Abstracts; EBSCOhost Products; ISI: Current Contents/Social & Behavioral Sciences, Social Sciences Citation Index, Research Alert, Social SciSearch; CINAHL;* and *Cumulative Index to Nursing and Allied Health Literature.*

Microform Copies: Microform copies of this journal are available through ProQuest Information and Learning, P.O. Box 1346, Ann Arbor, MI 48106–1346. For more information, call 1–800–521–0600, ext. 2888.

Visit LEA's website at **http://www.erlbaum.com**

Printed in the United States of America   ISSN 0899–5605

MILITARY PSYCHOLOGY, 2003, *15*(3), 163–166

Organizational Commitment in the Military: An Overview

Paul A. Gade
U.S. Army Research Institute

The military needs committed service members and families. We hear this all the time, but what does it mean to be a committed service member or spouse? Committed to what? And why do we want committed service members and spouses?

Generally, when we talk about a committed service member, we mean a person who is strongly attached to his or her military service as an organization and to his or her unit as part of that organization. We want committed soldiers and families because we expect them to perform their work better, to be more likely to stay in the military, and to be good citizens of their organizations.

How, then, do we define organizational commitment? Can we measure the amount of commitment people have to organizations? Can we determine the effect that organizational commitment has on performance and retention? Do we know what causes someone to be committed to an organization? These and other questions about organizational commitment have concerned researchers for several decades (see, for example, Mathieu & Zajac, 1990; Mowday, Porter, & Steers, 1982). In the most comprehensive look at organizational commitment to date, Meyer and Allen (1997) summarized much of this research and formulated a three-component theory of organizational commitment. They found that organizational commitment can be measured reliably using scaled items in a questionnaire. Further, they theorized, and in some cases showed, that such measures can be related to important outcomes, such as performance and retention in civilian organizations. Because we believe that the Meyer and Allen theory is the most well-developed and comprehensive theory of organizational commitment available to date, we have used it to organize the integration of the articles in this special issue.

Meyer and Allen (1997) defined organizational commitment as a combination of three component processes: *affective commitment* (AC), *continuance commit-*

Requests for reprints should be sent to Paul A. Gade, U.S. Army Research Institute, 5001 Eisenhower Avenue, Alexandria, VA 22333-5600. E-mail: gade@ari.army.mil.

ment (CC), and *normative commitment* (NC). AC is the *want to* of commitment. It represents a soldier's or a spouse's emotional attachment to, or identification with, the military service or the unit. CC is the *need to* aspect of commitment. For example, a soldier or spouse feels the need to continue in the military because it would be hard to find another job or because he or she has too many years invested in the military to leave. NC is the *ought to* of commitment. This represents a soldier's or a spouse's felt obligation to remain with the organization; either may see the Army as a moral obligation or "calling," not merely a job. In summary, organizational commitment can be viewed as a composite measure of various types of motives for remaining with, and performing for, an organization. In this sense, most military personnel and organizational research is about measuring service member commitment to the military in some fashion.

Most military researchers who have attempted to measure organizational commitment have done so on an ad hoc basis, preferring to invent new items and scales rather than incorporate well-established measures, such as those of Meyer and Allen (1997), that have strong theoretical underpinnings. The purpose of this special issue is to reverse this trend by bringing military organizational commitment research into the scientific mainstream in ways that will prove useful to military services and advance organizational commitment theory and knowledge.

This special issue grew out of an organizational commitment measurement symposium conducted at the August 1998 annual American Psychological Association (APA) convention in San Francisco. The need for that symposium arose when many of us, through our independent research efforts, recognized the potential practical importance of measuring organizational commitment and maintaining a healthy concern for ensuring that this measurement was well-grounded in organizational commitment theory. It is to these ends that this special issue is dedicated.

The first article, by Tremble, Payne, Finch, and Bullis opened the door to exploiting archived data collected using ad hoc or "analog" measures of organizational commitment. By concurrently administering these ad hoc items with items from scales defined by Meyer and Allen (1997) and conducting confirmatory factor analyses, the authors were able to link these empirically based items to Meyer and Allen's measures of AC and CC.

The second article, by Gade, Tiggle, and Schumm looked at the psychometric properties of soldiers' responses to AC and CC scales by Meyer and Allen (1997) and examined the dimensionality of a short form of AC and CC scales derived from them. In addition, modified forms of these short scales were used to measure U.S. Army Reserve spouse commitment. The measurement of spouse commitment is particularly important to the military because spouse desire for the service member's career has been shown to be as important as that of the service member in determining actual retention behavior (Segal & Harris, 1993). This study also attempted to make connections between reliably measured AC and CC and retention and performance outcomes that are of practical importance to the military and of theoretical importance in establishing AC and CC construct validity.

The third article, by Heffner and Gade examined the differences in AC and CC between commitment of military men to Special Operations in particular and the military in general within the framework of Lawler's theory of nested collectives (Lawler, 1992). This article explored the allegiance and commitment of elite service members to their special organizations and how this commitment to Special Operations may have influenced their commitment to the military in general. The short form for measuring commitment (Gade et al.) was used to measure the commitment of Special Operations personnel in the Army, Navy, and Air Force.

The fourth article, by Karrasch is the only article in this special issue that attempted to account for potential organizational commitment antecedents. This study examined gender, ethnicity, branch of the Army, and perceptions of tokenism as possible antecedents of AC, CC, and NC. This study also investigated the relation of these potential antecedents of commitment, and the commitment measures themselves, to peer-rated leadership performance as an outcome variable.

Taken together, these four articles have demonstrated the robustness of Meyer and Allen's (1997) concepts of AC and CC and their underlying measures by using them in very different military samples, including spouses, and under a variety of operational conditions. Furthermore, these constructs hold up extremely well when measured with a reduced number of items. Perhaps most significantly, these four studies demonstrated that both AC and CC are important for predicting and understanding outcomes that are vital to military organizations, such as attrition, morale, and performance.

However, some of us, including me, had abandoned the concept of NC prematurely because its measures tend to correlate so highly with AC measures. Because of its potential utility for predicting and explaining military performance and readiness, we need to try a little harder to measure this construct in our military populations. The military, of all organizations, should be the ideal place to explore this concept. If NC cannot be demonstrated in the military services, I doubt it can be demonstrated anywhere.

Rounding out this special issue is a pithy discussion that ties together the practical and theoretical significance of the four studies presented here (Allen). It was our good fortune that Natalie Allen graciously consented to take on this task during her very busy sabbatical leave in England and Australia. In addition to Dr. Allen's discussion of our articles, all of the special issue authors have benefited greatly from her keen insights and helpful suggestions on earlier drafts of our articles. Our final products are far better as a result.

Although we collected, shaped, and melded these articles into the symposium and subsequent special issue, the research underlying our articles was not part of a comprehensive investigation of Army organizational commitment. Although organizational commitment was an important part of each study, it was not its central theme in most cases. Rather, by bringing these studies together in this special issue, we hope to encourage just such an integrated effort to study the measurement, significant consequences, and antecedents of organizational commitment for all military services.

I would be remiss if I did not thank the three reviewers of this special issue for their time, effort, and especially for their cogent suggestions. Their recommended revisions have made each of our articles stronger, more understandable, and more relevant. We owe all of them a great debt.

I also want to thank Janice Laurence for her help and guidance in making this special issue both possible and desirable. Finally, I want to thank the founding editor, Marty Wiskoff, for encouraging us to develop this special issue after our 1998 APA symposium.

Paul A. Gade
Guest Editor

ACKNOWLEDGMENTS

The views, opinions, and/or findings contained in this article are solely those of the author and should not be construed as an official Department of the Army or DOD position, policy, or decision, unless so designated by other documentation.

REFERENCES

Allen, N. J. (2003/this issue). Organizational commitment in the military: A discussion of theory and practice. *Military Psychology, 15,* 237–253.

Gade, P. A., Tiggle, R. B., & Schumm, W. (2003/this issue). The measurement and consequences of military organizational commitment in soldiers and spouses. *Military Psychology, 15,* 191–207.

Heffner, T. S., & Gade, P. A. (2003/this issue). Commitment to nested collectives in Special Operations Forces. *Military Psychology, 15,* 209–223.

Karrasch, A. I. (2003/this issue). Antecedents and consequences of organizational commitment. *Military Psychology, 15,* 225–236.

Lawler, E. J. (1992). Affective attachment to nested groups: A choice process theory. *American Sociological Review, 57,* 327–339.

Mathieu, J. E., & Zajac, D. M. (1990). A review and meta-analysis of the antecedents, correlates, and consequences of organizational commitment. *Psychological Bulletin, 108,* 171–194.

Meyer, J. P., & Allen, N. J. (1997). *Commitment in the workplace: Theory, research, and application.* Thousand Oaks, CA: Sage.

Mowday, R. T., Porter, L. W., & Steers, R. M. (1982). Employee-organization linkages: The psychology of commitment, absenteeism, and turnover. New York: Academic.

Segal, M. W., & Harris, J. J. (1993). *What we know about Army families* (Special Rep. No. 21). Alexandria, VA: U.S. Army Research Institute for the Behavioral and Social Sciences. (DTIC No. AD–A271 989)

Tremble, T. R., Jr., Payne, S. C., Finch, J. F., & Bullis, R. C. (2003/this issue). Opening organizational archives to research: Analog measures of organizational commitment. *Military Psychology, 15,* 167–190.

MILITARY PSYCHOLOGY, 2003, *15*(3), 167–190

Opening Organizational Archives to Research: Analog Measures of Organizational Commitment

Trueman R. Tremble, Jr.
U.S. Army Research Institute for the Behavioral and Social Sciences

Stephanie C. Payne and John F. Finch
Texas A&M University

R. Craig Bullis
United States Military Academy

This research applied the construct equivalence approach for deriving and empirically validating analog measures based on data not originally designed to measure the theoretical constructs of interest. In this application, subject matter experts agreed on questionnaire items from a longitudinal database that fit Meyer and Allen's (1991) definitions of affective and continuance commitment. Questionnaires suitable for inclusion of these items and the original Meyer and Allen (1984) items were administered to a test sample of Army officers ($N = 404$). Analyses supported use of the selected items as analog scales of affective and continuance commitment in that both the selected and original items yielded similar factor structures and similar relations with officer rank and career intentions. Results for the analog items were replicated with another officer sample ($N = 863$). The contributions of the findings to the organizational commitment literature and research in the military are discussed.

The Army has a need to develop and maintain a force of soldiers for military service who are highly motivated and capable. This need is partly derived from the unique conditions of military service, which can involve a life requiring travel (including deployments away from family members), frequent relocation as well as

Requests for reprints should be sent to Trueman R. Tremble, Jr., U. S. Army Research Institute for the Behavioral and Social Sciences, ATTN: TAPC-ARI-RS, 5001 Eisenhower Avenue, Alexandria, Virginia 22333-5600. E-mail may be sent to: tremble@ari.army.mil.

temporary duty assignments, and selflessness in the execution of life-threatening duties. *Organizational commitment* is a construct potentially useful for characterizing and understanding willing and active military service of soldiers despite the associated hardships. It has been generally viewed as a complex construct involving acceptance of organizational values, willingness to put forth effort for the organization, and desire for continued membership.

Empirical results have shown the utility of organizational commitment for understanding the behavior of members of organizations. Meta-analyses have demonstrated that organizational commitment is consistently related to variables associated with withdrawal from the organization, to include perceived job alternatives, intention to search, intention to leave, lateness, absenteeism, and turnover (Griffeth, Hom, & Gaertner, 2000; Mathieu & Zajac, 1990).

Although the negative consequences that result from low levels of organizational commitment are quite clear, how individuals become committed to their organization and how this construct develops over time remains less certain. The best way to answer these questions may be through longitudinal research. Over the past decade, the Army has assembled a data archive potentially suitable for such longitudinal research. This archive contains thousands of responses to survey items about career decision making. Unfortunately, it does not contain standard measures of organizational commitment. Absence of such measures has limited the research value of the archive by reducing certainty about the meaning of findings from the data and their relation to the wider body of research. To make use of this archive, the validity of the survey items needed to be established. Accordingly, the purpose of this research was to develop and validate analog scales of organizational commitment for use with the Army archive.

ORGANIZATIONAL COMMITMENT

Meyer and Allen (1991) defined organizational commitment as "a psychological state that (a) characterizes the employee's relationship with the organization and (b) has implications for the decision to continue membership in the organization" (p. 67). Allen and Meyer (1990) distinguished among three components of organizational commitment and developed and validated measures for each. These components differ in terms of the sources of attraction for relationship with the organization and are referred to as *affective commitment* (AC), *continuance commitment* (CC), and *normative commitment* (NC). This study focuses primarily on AC and CC.[1]

---

[1]The sources of attraction distinguishing the components of commitment seem to bear some similarity to distinctions among social influence based on compliance, identification, and internalization (Deutsch & Gerard, 1955; Kelman, 1958).

"Affective commitment refers to the employee's emotional attachment to, identification with, and involvement in the organization" (Meyer & Allen, 1997, p. 11). This component of commitment may encourage adherence to the expectations and values of the organization and positively relates to tenure in the organization (Mathieu & Zajac, 1990). "Continuance commitment refers to an awareness of the costs associated with leaving the organization" (Meyer & Allen, 1997, p. 11). This component of commitment has been associated with the side bets or investments an employee makes with an organization. It has been found to be less stable than AC over time (Gade, Tiggle, & Schumm, 2003/this issue).

Meyer and Allen (1997) indicated that AC develops within individuals as organizational experiences satisfy their needs, meet their expectations, and allow for goal achievement. Commissioned officers in the Army are likely to have such experiences as their role is to shape goals and direct activities to attain assigned military missions. Accordingly, the AC component seems to fit with the traditional view of the professional soldier more so than the CC component.

Meyer and Allen's Affective and Continuance Commitment Scales

In a review of over 40 studies that employed their scales, Allen and Meyer (1996) reported acceptable median reliabilities (internal consistencies) of .85 and .79 for their AC and CC scales, respectively. Further evidence of construct validity has been obtained in both exploratory (Allen & Meyer, 1990; McGee & Ford, 1987; Reilly & Orsak, 1991) and confirmatory factor analyses (Meyer, Allen, & Gellatly, 1990; Moorman, Niehoff, & Organ, 1993; Shore & Tetrick, 1991), including studies with samples of Army officers (e.g., Oliver, Tiggle, & Hayes, 1996; Teplitsky, 1991). These studies have consistently demonstrated that the AC and CC items differentially load on separate factors and that AC is a unidimensional scale. Results have been less clear about the dimensionality of CC. Both exploratory analyses (McGee & Ford, 1987) and confirmatory analyses (Bullis & Wong, 1994; Dunham, Grube, & Castaneda, 1994; Hackett, Bycio, & Hausdorf, 1994; Magazine, Williams, & Williams, 1996; Somers, 1993) have suggested separation of the CC items into two continuance subscales, one composed of the items concerning available alternatives (CC_{alt}) and the other composed of items describing the personal sacrifices created by leaving the organization (CC_{sac}). In fact, Meyer et al. (1990) also found empirical support for this separation. More recently, however, Meyer and Allen (1997) described the dimensionality of CC as an "unresolved issue" in which the utility of the subscales is questionable.

Meyer and Allen's (1984) AC and CC scales have also produced the pattern of prediction found in the wider literature on commitment. For example, all three of Meyer and Allen's scales have correlated negatively with turnover intentions, with AC producing a relatively stronger association (Hackett et al., 1994; Meyer, Allen,

& Smith, 1993; Meyer, Stanley, Herscovitch, & Topolnytsky, 2002). This demonstrates the value of distinguishing among forms of commitment.

Meyer and Allen's (1984) measures have been used in several studies concerning the career intentions of Army soldiers. For example, Oliver et al. (1996) surveyed 503 Army soldiers in an attempt to identify the "before deployment status" of reserve soldiers who had volunteered for an overseas deployment. Nearly 88% of this sample of volunteers reported intentions to remain in the Army for the duration of a full career (20 years of service) and expressed strong levels of both AC and CC. In another Army study, Teplitsky (1991) predicted an officer's "propensity to stay" in the Army using Meyer and Allen's AC scale. A significant path coefficient was found between AC and propensity to stay in the Army, suggesting that officers with high levels of AC were more inclined to remain in the Army beyond their initial obligation than officers with lower levels of AC.

Longitudinal Studies of Organizational Commitment

It has been suggested that the development of organizational commitment is a gradual process (Mowday, Porter, & Steers, 1982). In fact, Mathieu and Zajac (1990) emphasized a need for research that determines "how organizational commitment develops over time and what factors are most critical to employees at various career stages" (p. 191). Allen and Meyer (1996) also advocated developmental research to determine how to measure commitment over time. Based on these views, longitudinal studies appear to hold promise for understanding the development of organizational commitment and for determining its antecedents, consequences, and measurement.

Although several longitudinal studies of organizational commitment have been conducted (e.g., Bateman & Strasser, 1984; Fisher, 1985; Meyer & Allen, 1987; Mowday & McDade, 1979, 1980; Mowday et al., 1982; Pierce & Dunham, 1987; Porter, Crampon, & Smith, 1976; Porter, Steers, Mowday, & Boulian, 1974; Van Maanen, 1975; Werbel & Gould, 1984), the longitudinal period covered did not typically exceed 12 months. Evidence suggests that longer tracking periods may be needed to reap the benefits of longitudinal research. Mowday et al. (1982), for example, found that personnel entering an organization undergo an initial socialization period and that the factors determining commitment are likely to change over the course of this time period. In a sample of police officers, Van Maanen (1975) similarly found that organizational commitment did not stabilize before 30 months of employment.

As indicated earlier, the Army has assembled a data archive potentially suitable for longitudinal research on the development of the organizational commitment of commissioned officers. This archive was produced through mail surveys administered during the period of 1988 to 2000 and as part of a research program on officer careers and their families known earlier as Longitudinal Research on Officer Careers (LROC) and later as the Survey of Officer Careers (SOC). Despite some variation, there was considerable continuity in the questionnaire items in the seven survey administrations. In all surveys, questionnaire items sought officers' views on a number of practical issues, including career decision making. The irony of this is that, even though item consistency allows for comparisons over time, it perpetuates the problem of not having standard measures of psychological constructs available to answer research questions. Several reports have described the purpose and preliminary results of the surveys (Harris, 1994; Harris, Wochinger, Schwartz, & Parham, 1993; McCloy, Laurence, & DiFazio, 1996). As described in these reports, the LROC–SOC data have been formed into an archive ready for use in longitudinal research, studies, and analyses.

A review of questionnaire items revealed that several seemed to fit well with the content domains of Meyer and Allen's (1984) AC and CC. This fit suggested the possibility of applying a construct equivalence approach to the LROC–SOC archive. According to this approach, which is based on Cronbach and Meehl's (1955) construct validity theory, data existing in organizational archives can be transformed into "analog" or surrogate measures of behavioral constructs that are set forth in theory and have accepted measures. With valid transformation, the organizational archives become useful for study of the constructs measures and the theories testable by the analog measures.

APPLICATION OF THE CONSTRUCT EQUIVALENCE
APPROACH

According to the construct equivalence approach, data already existing in an archive and likely to be useful for measuring a construct are selected. Statistical procedures are then applied to determine how to combine or transform the data into a measure of the construct. Using samples with data available on both the selected archival items and a standard measure of the construct, the descriptive and predictive properties of the measure derived from the archival data are compared with those of the standard measure. The derived measure is treated as an "analog" of the standard measure when the analog measure produces results that are similar to the standard measure in terms of both descriptive and predictive properties. For more information on this approach, see Payne, Finch, and Tremble (in press).

Following this approach, three military researchers reviewed LROC–SOC questionnaires. The researchers identified the items common to the survey administrations across years. They also reached consensus that six and seven items reflected Meyer and Allen's (1991) definitions of AC and CC, respectively. Close inspection showed that, like the items in the original CC scale, three of the selected items reflected sacrifices, and four items concerned available alternatives. The expectation was that the average of responses to the items selected for a Meyer and Allen commitment component could serve as an analog scale for measuring that construct.

To test this, five conditions required for construct equivalence were examined: (a) More specifically, the analog items were expected to demonstrate a similar factor structure to Meyer and Allen's (1984) items; (b) when administered together, the analog and original scales were expected to produce similar levels of central tendency and dispersion; (c) the analog scales were also expected to demonstrate similar levels of reliability to the original scales (d) as well as convergent and divergent validity by correlating more strongly with the original counterpart (AC or CC) than the other; (e) finally, relations observed in previous studies should hold for both the analog and original scales. The specific hypotheses to be tested here were:

1. In samples of military commissioned officers, affective commitment is stronger than continuance commitment.
2. Employee longevity is more strongly related to affective commitment than continuance commitment.
3. Career intentions are more strongly related to affective commitment than continuance commitment.

Meyer and Allen's (1984) AC and CC items and the candidate analog items were included in the questionnaires administered to the Army officers participating in two projects investigating commitment. The construct validity of the analog scales was also examined by testing the three previously stated hypotheses, which were based on results of past research on commitment and their applicability to the officer samples. In addition, the same three hypotheses were examined with responses from a sample of officers drawn from the LROC–SOC data set, which was targeted for eventual application of the analog scales. The selected target sample was longitudinal and consisted of the officers who had completed LROC–SOC questionnaires at each of three time periods between 1988 and 1996. This permitted confirmation of results comparing the Meyer and Allen and analog scales prior to their fuller application in the LROC–SOC. In summary, the construct equivalence approach was applied. Support for scales derived from the LROC–SOC archive in accordance with the conditions of this approach was considered evidence for use of the scales as analog stand-ins for the original Meyer and Allen scales.

METHOD

Participants

Two samples of commissioned Army officers served as participants in this research. We refer to these as the test sample and the target sample.

TABLE 1
Summary of Administered Commitment Items

Meyer and Allen (1984) Affective Commitment	*Analog Affective Commitment*
1. I really feel as if the Army's problems are my own.	1. Civilians are more likely to share my values and beliefs than other officers.[a]
2. The Army has a great deal of personal meaning for me.	2. One of the things I value most about the Army is the sense of community or camaraderie I feel.
3. I enjoy discussing the Army with people outside it.	3. I would discourage a close friend from joining the Army.[a]
4. I do not feel "emotionally attached" to the Army.[a]	4. I can count on Army people to help out when needed.
5. I do not feel a strong sense of belonging in the Army.[a]	5. I am quite proud to tell people I am in the Army.
6. I do not feel like "part of the family" in the Army.[a]	6. I feel I am really a part of the Army organization.
7. I think I could easily become as attached to another organization as I am to the Army.[a]

Meyer and Allen (1984) Continuance Commitment	*Analog Continuance Commitment*
1. I am not afraid of what might happen if I quit the Army without another job lined up.[a] (Alt)	1. It would be difficult for me to find a good civilian job right now, considering my own qualifications and current labor market conditions.
2. Too much of my life would be disrupted if I decided I wanted to leave the Army now.	2. The overall standard of living is better in the military, compared to a civilian job that I could realistically expect to get. (Alt)
3. It wouldn't be too costly for me to leave the Army in the near future.[a]	3. It would be difficult for me to leave the Army in the next year or so, given my current personal or family situation.
4. One of the major reasons I may stay in the Army is that leaving would require considerable personal sacrifice — another organization may not match the overall benefits I have.	4. The opportunities to advance are better in the military, compared to a civilian job that I could realistically expect to get. (Alt)
5. It would be very hard for me to leave the Army right now, even if I wanted to.	5. It would be difficult for me financially to be unemployed for 2 or 3 months if I needed time to find a new job.
6. I feel I have too few options to consider leaving the Army. (Alt)	6. The overall quality of life is better in the military, compared to a civilian job that I could realistically expect to get. (Alt)
7. Right now, staying in the Army is a matter of necessity as much as a desire. (Alt)	7. Personal freedom is better in the military, compared to a civilian job that I could realistically expect to get. (Alt)
8. One of the few negative consequence s of leaving the Army would be the scarcity of available alternatives. (Alt)

Note. Alt = Continuance commitment low alternative items. [a]Reverse coded items.

173

Test sample.   The test sample combined the samples of officers who participated in two separate studies, for a total of 404 officers. The first subsample comprised 278 officers stationed at an Army post a few months prior to post inactivation. This subsample responded to a mail questionnaire on Army restructuring. The questionnaire was originally mailed to 550 officers and warrant officers, of which 312 responded for a response rate of 57%. The sample was reduced to the 278 commissioned officers who responded to the survey.

The second subsample consisted of 126 battalion staff officers distributed across 47 battalions. This second subsample responded to a questionnaire on leadership and organizational decision processes at their respective posts (see Tremble, Kane, & Stewart, 1997). Initially, researchers requested four battalion staff officers from 53 battalions for a total of 212 officers. A total of 144 responded for a response rate of 68%. The sample was reduced to the 126 commissioned officers who reported their rank when responding to the survey.

In the total test sample, 83% were men and 82% were White. Officer rank ranged from second lieutenant to colonel, with a modal rank of captain (42%). On average, the officers had completed 9 years of service in the Army.

Target sample.   The target sample consisted of the 863 Army officers who completed the LROC–SOC questionnaire on three separate occasions: 1988, 1992, and 1996. Officers in this sample were primarily men (78%) and White (87%). In 1988 the officers were on average 28 years of age, held the rank of captain (68%), and had completed 5 years of service in the Army. As the samples consisted of the same officers for all 3 years, demographic variables associated with time (e.g., age, rank) tended to increase across the three periods.

Instruments

Table 1 summarizes the original Meyer and Allen (1984) items administered to the test sample and the analog questionnaire items administered to both the test sample and the target sample in all 3 years. Consistent with other Army research (Oliver et al., 1996; Teplitsky, 1991), participants were administered seven of the eight Meyer and Allen AC items and all eight of the CC items.[2]

These items were modified to state "the Army" instead of "my organization." For the test sample, the commitment items were intermingled among other questionnaire items and were formatted to retain, as much as possible, their original presentation but also to fit with the questionnaire of which they were a part. With one exception, test and target participants responded to an item by choosing from a

----

[2]The omitted Meyer and Allen AC item was "I would be happy to spend the rest of my career in this organization." It was believed that this item confounded the criterion of interest (career intent) with the intended predictor (AC).

5-point Likert-type scale with anchors ranging from *strongly agree* to *strongly disagree*. The exception involved the first test subsample. That subsample used a 7-point Likert-type scale to express agreement with the analog alternatives items. Responses on the 7-point scale were systematically reduced to a 5-point scale prior to further data analysis.[3]

Officers also responded to a single item similar to items used in previous Army research to measure career intent (e.g., Bullis & Wong, 1994; Oliver et al., 1996; Teplitsky, 1991). This item read: "Which of the following best describes your career intentions at the present time?" Officers responded to this question on a 5-, 6-, or 9-point scale (depending on the questionnaire completed) ranging from "I will definitely leave the Army [before/on] completion of my present obligation" to "I will definitely stay in the Army until retirement." Although multi-item scales are preferred over single-item measures, a recent meta-analysis examining the relation between single-item and scale measures of job satisfaction demonstrated the acceptability of single-item measures when "the research question implies their use or when situational constraints limit or prevent the use of scales" (Wanous, Reichers, & Hudy, 1997, p. 250; see also Wanous & Hudy, 2001).

Procedure

For the test sample, data collection procedures varied by the study in which the officers had participated. The 278 officers remaining at the post undergoing inactivation received by mail a 122-item survey concerning the effects of post inactivation on the organizational commitment of survivors (officers with reassignments to other elements of the Army). Officers completed the questionnaire on their own time and returned it to a centralized Army survey office. The questionnaire and its administration were designed to ensure anonymity. Civilian researchers administered the 160-item questionnaire to the 126 battalion staff officers during in-class sessions held at the officers' stations or posts. One session was held for each of the 47 battalions sampled. Staff officers participated along with other members of their units. Administration emphasized response confidentiality, as opposed to participant anonymity.

For the target sample, stratified random samples of company-grade officers commissioned from 1980 through the preceding survey year were mailed the LROC–SOC surveys (see Harris, 1994, for a more complete description of the sampling methodology used in the LROC). Officers completed the surveys on their own time and returned them to a centralized Army survey office. Response rates for the years of interest were as follows: 5,598 out of 8,931 (63%), 4,563 out of 9,674 (47%), and 10,240 out of over 22,000 (approximately 47%) for Times 1–3,

---

[3]Responses originally scored 1–7 were reassigned values as follows: 1 = 1, 2 = 1.67, 3 = 2.33, 4 = 3, 5 = 3.67, 6 = 4.33, and 7 = 5.

respectively. The 863 officers who provided usable responses to all three surveys were used as the target sample in the investigation reported here.

RESULTS

The analyses reported in this section begin with the test sample and end with the target sample. As appropriate, the same analyses were performed on each sample. Analyses focused on five conditions of construct equivalence and the three hypotheses previously proposed.

Test Sample: Factor Structure of Commitment Items

To examine the factor structure of the analog items (Condition 1), a confirmatory interbattery factor analysis was initially conducted. Although a number of approaches have been proposed for addressing interbattery effects within a confirmatory factor analysis (CFA) framework (see Marsh & Grayson, 1995), the most commonly used strategy specifies method factors whereby each measured variable loads on one trait factor and one method factor. One advantage of such a specification is that trait and method variance components are estimated separately, which readily facilitates the decomposition of variance into trait and method effects. In addition, correlations among method factors can be estimated, as can correlations between trait and method factors.

It was expected that dimensions representing Meyer and Allen's (1984) framework account for responses to the analog items. In other words, a two-factor measurement model comprising AC and CC was expected to fit the combined data (responses to Meyer and Allen's items and to the analog commitment items). In addition, a three-factor measurement model in which the subscales of CC (low alternatives and high sacrifices) loaded on separate factors was also examined. Each of these models was tested using confirmatory interbattery factor analysis with LISREL VIII (Jöreskog & Sörbom, 1996).

The following specifications were made for the two-factor measurement model: (a) the matrix of factor loadings was specified so each scale item had a nonzero loading on one factor, and the loadings on the other factor were constrained to equal zero; (b) error terms associated with scales from the same battery were correlated by freeing the appropriate off-diagonal elements in the matrix of measurement errors; and (c) because a weak, positive association was anticipated between the two commitment dimensions (Meyer et al., 1990), the covariance between the two latent constructs were specified as free to be estimated. In addition, to establish a metric for each latent construct, a marker-variable strategy was employed, whereby the unstandardized loading of one scale on each latent construct was fixed to a value of 1.0. Finally, following Panter, Tanaka, and Hoyle (1994), equality constraints were imposed on error variances of indicators of the same common factor. Collectively, these specifications represented a test of an interbattery factor model in which simple structure was imposed and battery-specific (method) variance was accounted for.

The fit of the two-factor interbattery model was satisfactory, as reflected by χ^2 $(189, N = 384) = 614.47, p < .001$, Comparative Fit Index = .89, Incremental Fit Index = .90. By comparison, the three-factor interbattery model yielded uninterpretable estimates and unacceptable fit. The maximum likelihood interbattery factor loadings for the two-factor model are presented in Table 2. Consistent with predictions, each manifest variable loaded significantly on its specified target factor (all $ps < .01$). As can be seen from Table 2, the standardized loadings ranged from .26 to .83, with neither the Meyer and Allen nor the analog scale dominating the solu-

TABLE 2
Confirmatory Interbattery Factor Loadings

Item	Factor 1	Factor 2
M&A AC 5	.69	
M&A AC 6	.68	
M&A AC 2	.68	
M&A AC 4	.67	
Analog AC 1	.66	
Analog AC 6	.62	
Analog AC 5	.55	
Analog AC 2	.55	
Analog AC 4	.52	
M&A AC 3	.52	
Analog AC 3	.48	
M&A AC 1	.43	
M&A AC 7	.30	
Analog CC 3		.67
M&A CC 7		.64
M&A CC 5		.62
Analog CC 5		.60
M&A CC 4		.60
M&A CC 1		.59
M&A CC 2		.58
Analog CC 1		.58
M&A CC 8		.57
M&A CC 6		.54
Analog CC 2		.47
Analog CC 6		.42
Analog CC 4		.40
M&A CC 3		.33
Analog CC 7		.26

Note. M&A = Meyer and Allen; AC = affective commitment; CC = continuance commitment.

tion. The first factor was defined primarily by Meyer and Allen's (1984) AC Item 2 ("The Army has a great deal of personal meaning for me"), Item 4 ("I do not feel 'emotionally attached' to the Army," reverse coded), Item 5 ("I do not feel a strong sense of belonging in the Army," reverse coded) and Item 6 ("I do not feel like 'part of the family' in the Army," reverse coded), and analog AC Item 1 ("Civilians are more likely to share my values and beliefs than other officers," reverse coded), and Item 6 ("I feel I am really a part of the Army organization"), reflecting the theme of AC. The second interbattery factor, which represented CC, was defined primarily by analog CC Item 3 ("It would be difficult for me to leave the Army in the next year or so, given my current personal or family situation") and Item 5 ("It would be difficult for me financially to be unemployed for 2 or 3 months if I needed time to find a new job"), and Meyer and Allen's CC Item 5 ("It would be very hard for me to leave the Army right now, even if I wanted to") and Item 7 ("Right now, staying in the Army is a matter of necessity as much as a desire"). Consistent with previous findings (e.g., Meyer et al., 1990), the correlation between the two interbattery factors was modest, although statistically significant ($r = .17, p < .05$).

Test Sample: Scale Development

Scales were developed separately for each of the two components of commitment for the original and analog items. Each commitment scale was calculated as the mean of the items administered for that scale. Prior to calculation, all items were coded so that higher scores reflected greater favor toward the construct. Descriptive statistics, scale reliabilities, and correlations between scale scores are reported in Table 3.

The data in Table 3 support further the construct equivalence between the analog and original scales. The means and standard deviations of the analog and original

TABLE 3
Test Sample: Descriptive Statistics and Correlations for Variables of Interest

	M	SD	1	2	3	4	5	6
1. Rank[a]	3.16	1.10	—					
2. Career Intent	3.82	1.03	.27**	—				
3. Meyer & Allen AC	3.67[b]	.69	.11*	.38**[d]	(.81)			
4. Analog AC	3.92[c]	.65	−.01	.32**[e]	.73**	(.75)		
5. Meyer & Allen CC	2.74[b]	.77	.04	.13**[d]	.17**	.10*	(.79)	
6. Analog CC	2.72[c]	.76	.08	.19**[e]	.24**	.20**	.70**	(.78)

Note. Reliabilities (coefficient alphas) are in parentheses on the diagonal. AC = affective commitment; CC = continuance commitment.

[a]1 = 2nd lieutenant, 6 = colonel. Variables noted with the same superscript are significantly different from each other. [b]$t_{(399)} = 20.01, p \leq .000.$ [c]$t_{(396)} = 26.51, p \leq .000,$ [d]$t = 4.21, p < .05,$ [e]$t = 2.61, p < .05.$
*$p < .05$, **$p < .01$.

scales were quite comparable (Condition 2), and the scale reliabilities were consistent with the median reliabilities reported in the studies reviewed by Allen and Meyer (1996; Condition 3). With respect to convergent validity, the two AC scales were significantly correlated with each other ($r = .73, p < .01$), and the two CC scales were significantly correlated with each other ($r = .70, p < .01$). The correlations across constructs (discriminant validity) were appreciably smaller (Condition 4).

Test Sample: Construct Relations

Hypothesis 1 stated that officers have higher levels of AC than CC. To test this, two dependent sample t tests were performed to determine if there were significant differences between the AC and CC scales. Support for this hypothesis was found for both commitment measures. As displayed in Table 3, the mean for the Meyer and Allen AC (1984) scale was 3.67, and the mean for the Meyer and Allen CC scale was 2.74, $t_{(399)} = 20.01, p = .000$. The mean for the analog AC scale was 3.92, and the mean for the analog CC scale was 2.72, $t_{(396)} = 26.51, p = .000$.[4]

The correlations between rank, career intent, and the four commitment scales for the test sample are also reported in Table 3. As might be expected, rank was significantly correlated with career intent ($r = .27, p < .01$). The expected relation between rank and AC was obtained when AC was measured with the Meyer and Allen (1984) AC scale ($r = .11, p = .026$) but not when it was measured with the analog AC scale ($r = -.01, p = .84$), providing partial support for Hypothesis 2, which stated that employee longevity is positively related to AC.

Career intent was significantly correlated with both types of commitment when they were measured either by the original scales or by the analog scales: AC (.38 and .32, respectively, $p < .01$) and CC (.13 and .19 respectively, $p < .01$). This suggests that the analog and original scales correlate similarly with other constructs (Condition 5). Consistent with Hypothesis 3, correlations between AC and career intent were significantly higher than correlations between CC and career intent for both the Meyer and Allen ($t = 4.21, p < .05$) and the analog measures ($t = 2.61, p < .05$).

To explore if AC predicted career intent above and beyond rank, two analyses of covariance (ANCOVAs) were conducted. After covarying out the effects of rank, results revealed main effects for both AC scales on career intent when each scale was examined individually.

Test Sample: Regression Analyses

To examine construct representation, four hierarchical multiple-regression analyses were performed. In all equations, career intent was the dependent variable. Re-

---

[4]Although the reported differences were obtained, their interpretation is not clear, given the scale transformations made to selected CC item responses.

sults are depicted in Table 4. When the Meyer and Allen (1984) AC scale was entered into the equation first ($R^2 = .15$), the analog AC scale *did not* add significantly to the equation. When the analog AC scale was entered into the equation first ($R^2 = .10$), the Meyer and Allen AC scale *did* add unique variance to the equation ($R^2 = .15$). Thus, the Meyer and Allen AC scale appeared to account for more variance in career intent than the analog AC scale. In contrast, the analog CC scale accounted for more variance than did the original CC scale. More specifically, when the Meyer and Allen CC scale was entered into the equation first ($R^2 = .02$), the analog CC scale *did* add unique variance to the equation ($R^2 = .04$). When the analog CC scale was entered into the equation first ($R^2 = .04$), the Meyer and Allen CC scale *did not* add significantly to the equation.

Target Sample: Factor Structure of Commitment Items

Results for the test sample suggested the promise for use of the analog scales in analyses of the LROC–SOC. As appropriate, the analyses conducted for the test sample were replicated with the target sample, drawn from the LROC–SOC, for further evidence on that promise.

As with the test sample, it was expected that dimensions representing Meyer and Allen's (1984) framework account for the target sample's responses to the analog items. Using LISREL VIII (Jöreskog & Sörbom, 1996), two- and three-factor models were tested using the data collected at each time period. Table 5 presents the results for the six CFAs. In all years, the three-component

TABLE 4
Test Sample: Hierarchical Regression Analyses for Career Intent

Variable	B	SE B	β	ΔR²	R²
Affective Commitment[a]					
1. Meyer & Allen AC	.573**	.070	.382	.146**	.146
2. Analog AC	.132	.108	.083	.003	.149
1. Analog AC	.505**	.076	.318	.101**	.101
2. Meyer & Allen AC	.482**	.102	.322	.048**	.149
Continuance Commitment[b]					
1. Meyer & Allen CC	.181*	.066	.136	.018*	.018
2. Analog CC	.257*	.094	.191	.018*	.037
1. Analog CC	.259**	.067	.192	.037**	.037
2. Meyer & Allen CC	.002	.093	.002	.000	.037

Note. For each of the four hierarchical regression analyses conducted to assess construct representation, this table lists and numbers the variables by step of entry, with regression outcomes (e.g., B weights) also summarized by step. AC = affective commitment, CC = continuance commitment.
    [a] $N = 398$. [b] $N = 396$
    *$p < .05$. **$p < .01$.

model specifying CC subcomponents (low alternatives and high sacrifices) was superior to the two-factor model. In fact, measures of goodness of fit for the three-factor models exceeded the threshold values recommended by Bagozzi and Yi (1988) with Adjusted Goodness Of Fit Indexes (AGFIs) of .95, .94, and .95 for Times 1–3, respectively. The phi matrices (Table 6) showed the expected pattern of divergence between the AC and CC factors and the expected pattern of convergence between the two CC factors (Condition 1). Results for the target sample suggest that Meyer and Allen's framework with the separation of CC into alternatives and sacrifices provides a basis for structuring and interpreting the analog commitment items. Given the continuit y of the target sample over three time periods, results for the target sample suggest further that Meyer and Allen's framework holds over a career period of 8 or more years.

TABLE 5
Target Sample: Summary of Confirmatory Factor Analyses

Model	χ^2	df	GFI	AGFI	RMSEA	NFI
Time 1 (1988)						
2-Factor Model	743.36*	64	.84	.78	.120	.62
3-Factor Model	162.46*	62	.97	.95	.047	.92
Time 2 (1992)						
2-Factor Model	782.80*	64	.83	.76	.120	.61
3-Factor Model	188.82*	62	.96	.94	.053	.91
Time 3 (1996)						
2-Factor Model	712.75*	64	.85	.79	.120	.66
3-Factor Model	180.20*	62	.96	.95	.051	.91

Note. 2-Factor Model = AC, CC;   3-Factor Model = AC, CC_{alt}, CC_{sac}); AC = affective commitment; CC = continuance commitment; CC_{alt} = continuance commitment, low alternatives; CC_{sac} = continuance commitment, high sacrifices, GFI = goodness of fit, AGFI = Adjusted Goodness Of Fit, RMSEA = root mean square error of approximation, NFI = Normed Fit Index.
[a]N=725; [b]N = 730; [c]N = 726
* $p < .05$

TABLE 6
Target Sample: Phi Correlation Matrices for Three-Factor
Confirmatory Models

	Time 1: 1988			Time 2: 1992			Time 3: 1996		
	1	*2*	*3*	*1*	*2*	*3*	*1*	*2*	*3*
1. AC	—		—	—		—			
2. CC_{alt}	.43*	—		.42*	—		.38*	—	
3. CC_{sac}	.10*	.19*	—	.07*	.17*	—	.11*	.22*	—

Note. AC = affective commitment; CC_{alt} = continuance commitment, low alternatives; CC_{sac} = continuance commitment, high sacrifices.
*$p < .05$.

Target Sample: Scale Development

Three analog commitment scales were computed for each of the higher order components of commitment: AC, CC_{alt}, and CC_{sac} at each time period. Each commitment scale was computed as the mean of the items administered for the scale. Descriptive statistics (Condition 2) and reliabilities (Condition 3) for all nine scales are reported in Table 7. Across the three time periods, the mean reliabilities were .71, .67, and .73 for the analog AC, CC_{alt}, and CC_{sac} scales, respectively. Although acceptable, these reliabilities were lower than ideal (Nunnally, 1978). Table 7, nevertheless, shows evidence for the convergent and discriminant validity of the analog scales (Condition 4). The discrimination was such that the correlations between measures of the same construct, but across time periods, were higher than the correlations across constructs and within (or across) time periods.

Target Sample: Construct Relations

Although results of scale comparisons are at best suggestive; three dependent sample t tests yielded evidence congruent with Hypothesis 1 that officers are significantly higher in AC than CC. As displayed in Table 7, the means for the AC scales were 4.02, 3.95, and 3.88 for the three successive time periods; corresponding means for the CC scales were 2.47, 2.60, and 2.32 for low alternatives and 2.75, 3.17, and 2.84 for high sacrifices.

The correlations between the commitment scales, organizational tenure, and career intent for the target sample are also reported in Table 7. Organizational tenure is displayed instead of rank for all three time periods, as it more directly describes employee longevity. Tenure also demonstrated more variance in the target sample than did rank. Despite this greater variance, support for Hypothesis 2 was weak. Only the measure of AC at Time 1 was significantly correlated with tenure, but the strength of this correlation coefficient was weak (about .09).

Support for Hypothesis 3 was again more consistent. At all three time periods, AC and CC_{alt} correlated significantly with career intent with one exception (the correlation between CC_{alt} at Time 1 and career intent at Time 3). CC_{sac} also correlated significantly with career intent in the corresponding year that it was measured. Consistent with Hypothesis 3 and previous findings (Hackett et al., 1994; Meyer et al., 1993, 2002), correlations between AC and career intent were significantly higher than correlations between CC_{alt} or CC_{sac} and career intent.[5]

As in the test sample, this relative difference held for correlations within the same time period (concurrent validity). In the target sample, this relative difference was also obtained across time periods (predictive validity; Condition 5).

[5]1988 CC_{alt} versus AC: $t = 2.86$; 1992 CC_{alt} versus AC: $t = 3.30$; 1996 CC_{alt} versus AC: $t = 3.21$; 1988 CC_{sac} versus AC: $t = 5.80$; 1992 CC_{sac} versus AC: $t = 3.90$; 1996 CC_{sac} versus AC: $t = 3.78$, all ps < .05.

TABLE 7
Target Sample: Means, Standard Deviations, and Correlations for the Commitment Scales, Organizational Tenure, and Career Intent

	M	SD	1	2	3	4	5	6	7	8	9	10	11	12	13	14	15
1. AC (1988)	4.02[ad]	0.49	0.71														
2. AC (1992)	3.95[be]	0.50	0.53	0.71													
3. AC (1996)	3.88[cf]	0.56	0.43	0.53	0.72												
4. CC: LoAlts (1988)	2.47[a]	0.73	0.29	0.20	0.11	0.68											
5. CC: LoAlts (1992)	2.60[b]	0.71	0.21	0.30	0.16	0.48	0.69										
6. CC: LoAlts (1996)	2.32[c]	0.73	0.11	0.19	0.28	0.38	0.43	0.65									
7. CC: HiSacs (1988)	2.75[d]	0.92	0.06	0.06	-.04	0.16	0.10	0.07	0.73								
8. CC: Hi Sacs (1992)	3.17[e]	0.92	0.03	0.05	-.04	0.08	0.09	0.03	0.57	0.73							
9. CC: HiSacs (1996)	2.84[f]	0.91	0.03	-.01	-.00	0.08	0.10	0.15	0.47	0.57	0.73						
10. Tenure (1988)	5.49	2.60	0.09	0.06	-.03	0.04	0.05	0.05	0.04	0.08	0.07	—					
11. Tenure (1992)	8.68	2.60	0.09	0.04	-.06	0.04	0.04	0.02	0.05	0.08	0.09	0.93	—				
12. Tenure (1996)	13.00	2.83	0.08	0.05	-.07	0.04	0.02	0.02	0.02	0.07	0.05	0.86	0.86	—			
13. Career Intent (1988)	4.80	1.06	0.38	0.22	0.12	0.27	0.15	0.08	0.12	0.09	0.05	0.37	0.38	0.35	—		
14. Career Intent (1992)	5.10	0.88	0.21	0.31	0.16	0.12	0.18	0.10	0.11	0.13	0.06	0.26	0.26	0.24	0.43	—	
15. Career Intent (1996)	5.14	0.95	0.15	0.18	0.29	0.06	0.10	0.17	0.02	0.02	0.11	0.31	0.30	0.26	0.28	0.34	—

Note. $N = 818$. Reliabilities (coefficient alphas) are on the diagonal. All correlations .07 or greater are significant ($p < .05$).

AC = affective commitment; CC = continuance commitment; LoAlts = low alternatives; HiSacs = high sacrifices.

Variables noted with the same superscript are significantly different from one another. [a]$t(853) = 60.69, p \le .000.$ [b]$t(852) = 53.57, p \le .000.$ [c]$t(849) = 57.53, p \le .000.$ [d]$t(861) = 36.21, p \le .000.$ [e]$t(859) = 22.39, p \le .000.$ [f]$t(859) = 28.63, p \le .000.$

183

Target Sample: Regression Analyses

As Table 7 shows, commitment and tenure were strongly correlated. To examine whether the analog scales accounted for variance in career intent above and beyond organizational tenure, three hierarchical multiple-regression analyses were performed (one for each time period). In all equations, organizational tenure was entered first, then AC, followed by CC_{alt}, and then CC_{sac}. As depicted in Table 8, the total amount of variance accounted for was 28%, 17%, and 17% for Times 1–3, respectively. For all 3 years, each of the three commitment scales predicted career intent above and beyond tenure. On average, tenure accounted for 9% of the variance, AC accounted for an additional 9% of the variance, and the CC components accounted for an additional 2% of the variance in career intent. These results further support Hypothesis 3, which proposed that AC is a stronger predictor of career intent than CC.

DISCUSSION

The analog scales seek to capitalize on and restructure existing organizational data files for use in research on broader theoretical issues. This study applied the con-

TABLE 8
Target Sample: Hierarchical Regression Analyses for Career Intent

Variable	B	SE B	β	ΔR^2	R^2
Time 1: 1988					
1. Organizational tenure	.148[**]	.013	.363	.131[**]	.131
2. Affective commitment	.736[**]	.064	.344	.118[**]	.249
3. Low alternatives	.255[**]	.045	.174	.028[**]	.277
4. High sacrifices	.008[*]	.034	.068	.004[*]	.281
Time 2: 1992					
1. Organizational tenure	.008[**]	.011	.244	.059[**]	.059
2. Affective commitment	.535[**]	.056	.302	.091[**]	.151
3. Low alternatives	.125[**]	.041	.101	.009[**]	.160
4. High sacrifices	.009[**]	.030	.104	.011[**]	.171
Time 3: 1996					
1. Organizational tenure	.009[**]	.011	.257	.066[**]	.066
2. Affective commitment	.506[**]	.054	.299	.089[**]	.155
3. Low alternatives	.118[**]	.043	.091	.008[**]	.163
4. High sacrifices	.009[**]	.033	.083	.007[**]	.169

Note. For each of the hierarchical regression analyses conducted to assess the contribution of commitment to reported career intent above organizational tenure, this table lists and numbers the variables by step of entry, with regression outcomes (e.g., *B* weights) also summarized by step.
[a]$N = 850$. [b]$N = 848$. [c]$N = 845$
[*]$p < .05$. [**]$p < .01$.

struct equivalence approach to a test sample and a target longitudinal sample to construct, validate, and further confirm scales for use in longitudinal research on organizational commitment. Results generally supported the analog scales as proxy measures of AC and CC. Despite their promise for research use, empirically derived scales risk both overrepresentation and underrepresentation of the constructs intended for measurement (Messick, 1995). With this reservation in mind, results of this development of analog scales add to the wider body of research on organizational commitment.

Test Sample Analyses

Results for the test sample altogether support the use of the analog scales in research on organizational commitment. The analog items formed the expected dimensions of AC and CC as indicated by results of the interbattery CFA. Representation of the AC and CC components was further indicated by the internal consistencies of the analog scales and by the convergence of measures around the expected construct (AC or CC) as opposed to convergence simply around method (original or analog).

In addition to forming the expected dimensions in the test sample, the analog scales generally performed like the original scales in predicting career intent. The one major difference in predictive validity of the analog and original scales was the correlation between rank and AC. Only the original AC scale was significantly but weakly correlated with rank.

Target Sample Analyses

Results for the target sample largely replicated and expanded those for the test sample. The confirmatory analyses supported the three-factor model of AC, CC_{alt}, and CC_{sac} at each data collection. This suggests stability of Meyer and Allen's (1984) framework and of the analog scales across an 8-year period (or longer) of organizational affiliation. This stability also appeared in the concurrent (within-data collections) and predictive (across-data collections) patterns of convergence and divergence between the AC and CC scales. Based on Table 7, this pattern was such that correlations between the same commitment component (AC or CC), but across the three time periods, were positive and moderately strong (ranging from .38 to .57); concurrent correlations between AC and CC were positive but weak (.00 to .29); and predictive relations between AC and CC, although remaining positive, were even weaker (.03 to .21).

Evidence of predictive validity also supports continued use of the analog scales in the target sample. Although both AC and CC were positively associated with career intent (Table 7), the concurrent and predictive associations were relatively stronger for AC than for CC. Contrary to previous research on civilian samples (Meyer et al.,

2002), CC_{alt} is more consistently correlated with career intent than CC_{sac}. This relation may be unique for Army officers or may reflect covariance with AC.

Construct Representation

Although results were promising, the regression analyses for the test sample revealed a disadvantage of the analog scales. That is, as argued earlier, analog scales have value when they "perform like" the originals. The regression analyses showed that the original and analog scales overlapped in their prediction of career intent, but the overlap was not complete. The lack of overlap was such that for any pair of scales, one scale explained variance over and above that explained by the other scale. For the AC scales, the stronger scale was the Meyer and Allen (1984) scale. The analog scale was the stronger CC predictor. Given these patterns, the analog AC scale seems to underrepresent the construct of affective commitment. This can also be a risk when using shortened or abbreviated scales. On the other hand, the analog CC scale seems to contain variance irrelevant to the construct of continuance commitment.

The imperfect representation of AC and CC by the analog scales limits their use in description as well as in prediction. Summary statistics could misrepresent the level of commitment of a sample. In Table 3, for example, it appears that although the directions of differences between AC and CC were consistent for both the analog and original scales, the analog AC scale described somewhat stronger levels of commitment than did the Meyer and Allen (1984) AC scale. Moreover, with misrepresentation of the content space, responses to individual analog items would be less useful for ascertaining the aspect of AC or CC commitment that is important for understanding a particular finding.

As mentioned earlier, however, separation of CC into CC_{alt} and CC_{sac} is not unique to the results here. Even the original CC items have not consistently demonstrated factor stability across studies. This lack of stability was obtained here in that, contrary to results for the target sample, only the two-factor model yielded an acceptable fit for the test sample. This inconsistency may call for measures that tap more directly into a psychological state of continuance as opposed to the conditions driving such a state. More generally, the inconsistency may call for clear separation of failures of theory from failures of its operationalization.

Implications

Although discipline in interpreting findings is warranted, the results for the test and target samples were consistent and have implications for the wider literature on organizational commitment and research in the military. With respect to the measurement of commitment, AC and CC appear to be distinguishable from each other. This is consistent with Allen and Meyer's (1996) review. Results for the target sample indicated robustness of the same factor structure across the approximately 8-year period of organizational affiliation by the officers in the sample.

This seems to suggest that Meyer and Allen's (1984) framework has promise for measuring and understanding organizational commitment over some portion of the duration of the career in an organization.

The findings here are also consistent with the wealth of the literature showing a relation between organizational commitment and career propensity, with the relation relatively stronger for AC than for CC (Allen & Meyer, 1996). These patterns characterized both the concurrent and predictive relations found in the target sample. Results for the target sample possibly raise questions about the stability of these patterns after longer periods of organizational membership. That is, despite the appearance of these patterns at all data collection intervals, the overall relations of AC and CC with career intent were somewhat weaker at the later intervals than at the earliest interval. This weakening appeared in the concurrent and predictive associations with career intent for both AC and CC (Table 7) and in the regression analyses for CC (Table 8). Continued deterioration of these relations over the career or over longer periods of organizational affiliation could have important implications for the meaning and measurement of organizational commitment.

Due to the longitudinal period covered, the LROC–SOC data offers a potentially unique opportunity for research on organizational commitment, its development, and measurement. The analog scales validated here represent two components of commitment studied in the wider literature, and their cautious use will help to realize the research potential of the LROC–SOC data set by linking and anchoring findings to Meyer and Allen's (1984) framework. Although analyses based on theory will contribute to the wider literature, it is important to recognize that this linkage also helps to strengthen certainty about implications for practical issues.

ACKNOWLEDGMENTS

A previous version of this article was presented at the 106th Annual Convention of the American Psychological Association, San Francisco, CA, August 1998.

R. Craig Bullis is now at the U.S. Army War College, Carlisle, PA.

The views, opinions, and/or findings contained in this article are solely those of the authors and should not be construed as an official Department of the Army or DOD position, policy, or decision, unless so designated by other documentation.

REFERENCES

Allen, N. J., & Meyer, J. P. (1990). The measurement and antecedents of affective, continuance, and normative commitment to the organization. *Journal of Occupational Psychology, 63,* 1–18.

Allen, N. J., & Meyer, J. P. (1996). Affective, continuance, and normative commitment to the organization: An examination of construct validity. *Journal of Vocational Behavior, 49,* 252–276.

Bagozzi, R. P., & Yi, Y. (1988). On the evaluation of structural equation models. *Journal of the Academy of Marketing Science, 16,* 74–94.

Bateman, T. S., & Strasser, S. (1984). A longitudinal analysis of the antecedents of organizational commitment. *Academy of Management Journal, 27,* 95–112.

Bullis, R. C., & Wong, L. (1994, August). *Career intentions and organizational commitment: Is what a manager influences significant?* Paper presented at the meeting of the Academy of Management, Dallas, TX.

Cronbach, L. J., & Meehl, P. E. (1955). Construct validity in psychological tests. *Psychological Bulletin, 52,* 281–302.

Deutsch, M., & Gerard, H. B. (1955). A study of normative and informational social influences upon individual judgment. *Journal of Abnormal and Social Psychology, 51,* 629–636.

Dunham, R. B., Grube, J. A., & Casteneda, M. B. (1994). Organizational commitment: The utility of an integrative definition. *Journal of Applied Psychology, 79,* 370–380.

Fisher, C. D. (1985). Social support and adjustment to work: A longitudinal study. *Journal of Management, 11,* 39–53.

Gade, P. A., Tiggle, R., & Schumm, W. R. (2003/this issue). The measurement and consequences of military organizational commitment in soldiers and spouses. *Military Psychology, 15,* 191–207.

Griffeth, R. W., Hom, P. W., & Gaertner, S. (2000). A meta-analysis of antecedents and correlates of employee turnover: Update, moderator tests, and research implications for the next millennium. *Journal of Management, 26,* 463–488.

Hackett, R. D., Bycio, P., & Hausdorf, P. (1994). Further assessments of Meyer and Allen's (1991) three-component model of organizational commitment. *Journal of Applied Psychology, 79,* 15–23.

Harris, B. C. (1994). *Perceptions of Army officers in a changing Army* (ARI Research Rep. No. 1662). Alexandria, VA: U.S. Army Research Institute for the Behavioral and Social Sciences. (DTIC No. AD–A 282 636)

Harris, B. C., Wochinger, K., Schwartz, J. P., & Parham, L. (1993). *Longitudinal research on officer careers: Vol. 1. Technical manual for 1988–1992 surveys* (ARI Research Product No. 93–10). Alexandria, VA: U.S. Army Research Institute for the Behavioral and Social Sciences. (DTIC No. AD–A 273 187)

Jöreskog, K. G., & Sörbom, D. (1996). *LISREL VIII: User's reference guide.* Chicago: Scientific Software International.

Kelman, H. C. (1958). Compliance, identification, and internalization: Three processes of attitude change. *Journal of Conflict Resolution, 2,* 51–60.

Magazine, S. L., Williams, L. J., & Williams, M. L. (1996). A confirmatory factor analysis examination of reverse coding effects in Meyer and Allen's affective and continuance commitment scales. *Educational and Psychological Measurement, 25,* 270–283.

Marsh, H. W., & Grayson, D. (1995). Latent variable models of multitrait-multimethod data. In R. H. Hoyle (Ed.), *Structural equation modeling: Concepts, issues and applications* (pp. 177–198). Newbury Park, CA: Sage.

Mathieu, J. E., & Zajac, D. M. (1990). A review and meta-analysis of the antecedents, correlates, and consequences of organizational commitment. *Psychological Bulletin, 108,* 171–194.

McCloy, R. A., Laurence, J. H., & DiFazio, A. S. (1996). *Monitoring the attitudes and perceptions of junior officers: The longitudinal research on officer careers (LROC) survey* (ARI Study Note No. 96–08). Alexandria, VA: U.S. Army Research Institute for the Behavioral and Social Sciences. (DTIC No. AD–A 320 598)

McGee, G. W., & Ford, R. C. (1987). Two (or more?) dimensions of organizational commitment: Reexamination of the affective and continuance commitment scales. *Journal of Applied Psychology, 72,* 638–642.

Messick, S. (1995). Validity of psychological assessment: Validation of inferences from persons' responses and performances as scientific inquiry into score meaning. *American Psychologist, 50,* 741–749.

Meyer, J. P., & Allen, N. J. (1984). Testing the "Side-Bet Theory" of organizational commitment: Some methodological considerations. *Journal of Applied Psychology, 69,* 372–378.

Meyer, J. P., & Allen, N. J. (1987). A longitudinal analysis of the early development and consequences of organizational commitment. *Canadian Journal of Behavioral Science, 19,* 199–215.

Meyer, J. P., & Allen, N. J. (1991). A three-component conceptualization of organizational commitment. *Human Resource Management Review, 1,* 61–98.

Meyer, J. P., & Allen, N. J. (1997). *Commitment in the workplace: Theory, research, and application.* Thousand Oaks, CA: Sage.

Meyer, J. P., Allen, N. J., & Gellatly, I. R. (1990). Affective and continuance commitment to the organization: Evaluations of measures and analysis of concurrent and time-lagged relations. *Journal of Applied Psychology, 75,* 710–720.

Meyer, J. P., Allen, N. J., & Smith, C. A. (1993). Commitment to the organizations and occupations: Extension and test of a three-component model. *Journal of Applied Psychology, 78,* 538–551.

Meyer, J. P., Stanley, D. J., Herscovitch, L., & Topolnytsky, L. (2002). Affective, continuance, normative commitment to the organization: A meta-analysis of antecedents, correlates, and consequences. *Journal of Vocational Behavior, 60,* 1–33.

Moorman, R. H., Niehoff, B. P., & Organ, D. W. (1993). Treating employees fairly and organizational citizenship behavior: Sorting the effects of job satisfaction, organizational commitment, and procedural justice. *Employee Responsibilities and Rights Journal, 6,* 209–225.

Mowday, R. T., & McDade, T. (1979, August). *Linking behavioral and attitudinal commitment: A longitudinal analysis of job choice and job attitudes.* Paper presented at the meeting of the Academy of Management, Atlanta, GA.

Mowday, R. T., & McDade, T. (1980, August). *The development of job attitude, job perceptions, and withdrawal propensities during the early employment period.* Paper presented at the annual meeting of the Academy of Management, Detroit, MI.

Mowday, R. T., Porter, L. W., & Steers, R. M. (1982). *Employee-organization linkages: The psychology of commitment, absenteeism, and turnover.* New York: Academic.

Nunnally, J. C. (1978). *Psychometric theory* (2nd ed.). NY: McGraw-Hill.

Oliver, L. W., Tiggle, R. B., & Hayes, S. M. (1996). *Preliminary report on selected life course variables and reasons for volunteering for the 28th Sinai deployment* (Army Tech. Rep. No. 1046). Alexandria, VA: U.S. Army Research Institute for the Behavioral and Social Sciences. (DTIC No. AD–A320 362)

Panter, A. T., Tanaka, J. S., & Hoyle, R. H. (1994). Structural models for multimode designs in personality and temperament research. In C. F. Halverson, G. A. Kohnstamm, & R. P. Martin (Eds.), *The developing structure of temperament and personality from infancy to adulthood* (pp. 111–138). Hillsdale, NJ: Lawrence Erlbaum Associates, Inc.

Payne, S. C., Finch, J. F., & Tremble, T. R., Jr. (in press). Validating surrogate measures of psychological constructs: The application of construct equivalence to archival data. *Organizational Research Methods.*

Pierce, J. L., & Dunham, R. B. (1987). Organizational commitment: Pre-employment prosperity and initial work experiences. *Journal of Management, 13,* 163–178.

Porter, L. W., Crampon, W. J., & Smith, F. J. (1976). Organizational commitment and managerial turnover: A longitudinal study. *Organizational Behavior and Human Performance, 15,* 87–98.

Porter, L. W., Steers, R. M., Mowday, R. T., & Boulian, P. V. (1974). Organizational commitment, job satisfaction, and turnover among psychiatric technicians. *Journal of Applied Psychology, 59,* 603–609.

Reilly, N. P., & Orsak, C. L. (1991). A career stage analysis of career and organizational commitment in nursing. *Journal of Vocational Behavior, 39,* 311–330.

Shore, L. M., & Tetrick, L. E. (1991). A construct validity study of the Survey of Perceived Organizational Support. *Journal of Applied Psychology, 76,* 637–643.

Somers, M. J. (1993). A test of the relationship between affective and continuance commitment using non-recursive models. *Journal of Occupational and Organizational Psychology, 66,* 185–192.

Teplitsky, M. L. (1991). *Junior Army officer retention intentions: A path analytic model* (Army Tech. Rep. No. 934). Alexandria, VA: U.S. Army Research Institute for the Behavioral and Social Sciences. (DTIC No. AD–A242 094)

Tremble, T. R., Jr., Kane, T. D., & Stewart, S. R. (1997). *A note on organizational leadership as problem solving.* (ARI Research Note No. 97–03) Alexandria, VA: U.S. Army Research Institute for the Behavioral and Social Sciences. (DTIC No. AD–A267 094)

Van Maanen, J. (1975). Police socialization: A longitudinal examination of job attitudes in an urban police department. *Administrative Science Quarterly, 20,* 207–228.

Wanous, J. P., & Hudy, M. J. (2001). Single-item reliability: A replication and extension. *Organizational Research Methods, 4,* 361–375.

Wanous, J. P., Reichers, A. E., & Hudy, M. J. (1997). Overall job satisfaction: How good are single-item measures? *Journal of Applied Psychology, 82,* 247–252.

Werbel, J. D., & Gould, S. (1984). A comparison of the relationship of commitment to turnover in recent hires and tenured employees. *Journal of Applied Psychology, 69,* 687–690.

The Measurement and Consequences of Military Organizational Commitment in Soldiers and Spouses

Paul A. Gade and Ronald B. Tiggle
U.S. Army Research Institute

Walter R. Schumm
Kansas State University

Based on the work of Meyer and Allen (1997), we derived a set of abbreviated scales to measure affective and continuance organizational commitment and conducted an extensive examination of the factor structure and reliability of these scales. The relation of these 2 abbreviated scales of organizational commitment to critical organizational outcomes was examined and tested. Results showed that affective and continuance commitment combined to influence subsequent soldier performance on job knowledge tests in opposite ways, suggesting a causal link between commitment and performance. Relations between affective and continuance commitment combinations and soldier-reported retention intentions, morale, and readiness were also explored. Scales developed to measure spouse commitment to the Army showed a factor structure that was comparable to that of soldiers and consistent with the dimensions of affective and continuance commitment.

Although organizational commitment is of vital concern to military organizations, there have been relatively few studies on organizational commitment conducted with military personnel. Using an organizational commitment scale developed by Porter and Smith (1970), Hom and Hulin (1981) assessed organizational commitment among more than 1,200 Army National Guard members. They found that organizational commitment successfully predicted both reenlistment intentions and reenlistment behavior. Later, Martin and O'Laughlin (1984) studied more than 1,200 Army reservists and found that affective commitment (AC) was related to

Requests for reprints should be sent to Paul A. Gade, U.S. Army Research Institute, 5001 Eisenhower Avenue, Alexandria, VA—22333-5600. E-mail: gade@ari.army.mil.

military job satisfaction, group (unit) cohesion, and retention intentions. Teplitzky (1991) used seven items from Meyer and Allen's (1984) measure of AC to measure organizational commitment in a study of retention among 714 junior officers in the Army. She found that AC was positively associated with a measure of career prospects and a measure of propensity to stay in the Army, although it was negatively related to anticipated job–family conflict in an Army career. She also found a small ($r = .17$) positive correlation between years of military service and AC. Rosen and Martin (1996) found that AC to the Army was correlated significantly with adjustment to Army life, perceived combat readiness, and psychological well-being in their survey of more than 1,300 soldiers from three different Army posts in the United States. Kim, Price, Mueller, and Watson (1996) found that AC predicted retention in a 1990 study of 244 Air Force physicians.

A growing body of evidence, well summarized by Meyer and Allen (1997), has shown that organizational commitment is a complex psychological state that may comprise several different components, each having distinct relations to behaviors of vital interest to the military services. There has been considerable support for the Meyer and Allen (1997) three-component—affective, continuance, and normative commitment—conceptualization of organizational commitment (see Dunham, Grube, & Castaneda, 1994, for examples). However, normative commitment (NC) has been shown to have considerable overlap with AC and continuance commitment (CC; Angle & Lawson, 1994; Brown, 1996; Hackett, Bycio, & Hausdorf, 1994). In contrast, the constructs of AC and CC are well established in the literature, although they may have been given other names by different researchers (e.g., attitudinal vs. calculative commitment, Mathieu & Zajac, 1990).

The research reported here had three goals. First, we wanted to assess the factor structure and reliability of affective and continuance organizational commitment scales, adapted from Meyer and Allen (1997), in a variety of military settings. Next, to ensure that military researchers easily could measure organizational commitment on a variety of military questionnaires, we wanted to develop shorter Meyer and Allen-based AC and CC scales and confirm their factor structure. And finally, we sought to demonstrate the utility of these measures for predicting outcomes important to the Army. Our research focused on AC and CC, excluding NC. We did this because current measures differentiate AC from CC very well, but NC overlaps considerably with AC, making it difficult to distinguish from AC even with sophisticated statistical techniques.

METHOD

Multinational Force and Observers (MFO) Samples and Materials

In 1993, the Chief of Staff of the Army, General Sullivan, tasked the active Army, the Reserve Components (RC—Army National Guard and Army Reserve), and the U.S. Army Research Institute to design a test for using RC volunteers to augment or replace active Army soldiers in the peacekeeping operation known as the Multinational Force and Observers (MFO). Known as the 28th MFO Rotation, a composite battalion task force of 518 soldiers was created from a mix of 20% active Army soldiers, 72% Army National Guard, and 8% Army Reserve soldiers. Ninety-nine percent of the composite battalion were men. Of the 5 female soldiers in the battalion, 3 were from the RC and 2 from the active Army. Details of the history and operation of the MFO and of this test and the demographics of its soldiers are given in Phelps and Farr (1996) and in Segal and Tiggle (1997).

Fall 1994.   This novel composite unit was formed at Ft. Bragg, North Carolina, and began training in the fall of 1994, was formally activated on November 4, 1994, and deployed for peacekeeping duties in the Sinai desert in January 1995. The unit remained on duty in the Sinai for the usual 6-month tour or rotation through June 1995, redeploying to Ft. Bragg where the unit was deactivated in July 1995. As part of the assessment design, the unit was surveyed on various topics on several occasions, and spouses of married soldiers in the unit were surveyed after deployment was completed. Seven affective and eight continuance organizational commitment items were administered as part of a background and training survey in the fall of 1994. These scales, adapted from those of Meyer and Allen (1984) and Allen and Meyer (1990), were designed to measure AC and CC (see Oliver, Tiggle, & Hayes, 1996, for a complete description of the items used). Four hundred ninety-nine of the 535 soldiers in the battalion completed all the organizational commitment items in that survey for a 93.3% usable response rate.

Spring 1995.   In May 1995 the soldiers were surveyed on a variety of attitudes and opinions about the MFO deployment while on duty in the Sinai. As part of this survey, the soldiers were given a test of general soldiering job knowledge and specific MFO peacekeeping job knowledge. This test consisted of 42 multiple-choice, general soldiering job knowledge items and 57 multiple-choice, MFO-specific job knowledge items. Further descriptions of these job knowledge tests can be found in Reynolds and Campbell (1996). Of the 480 enlisted soldiers and noncommissioned officers (NCOs), on duty in the Sinai in May 1995, 398 completed usable measures of general soldiering and MFO-specific job knowledge for a response rate of 82.9%. Of these, 239 RC soldiers provided both commitment measures from the fall of 1994 and job knowledge performance measures from May 1995 which were used to assess the relation between these two variables.

January of 1997.   After returning from the Sinai, soldiers and the spouses of married soldiers in the unit were surveyed via telephone on a variety of attitudes and opinions and given a shortened form of organizational commitment scales in January 1997. The shortened form of the commitment scales contained the following items for AC: (a) I feel like "part of the family" in the military; (b) the military has a great deal of personal meaning for me; (c) I feel a strong sense of belonging to the military; (d) I feel emotionally attached to the military. CC was measured using the following four items: (a) It would be too costly for me to leave the military in the near future; (b) I am afraid of what might happen if I quit the military; (c) too much in my life would be interrupted if I decided I wanted to leave the military; (d) one of the problems of leaving the military would be the lack of available alternatives. All items were measured using a 5-point Likert-type scale ranging from *strongly agree* to *strongly disagree,* with a midpoint of *neither agree nor disagree.* Preliminary address information could only be found for 490 soldiers who had deployed. We were able to locate and contact 341 of these soldiers. Four refused to participate in the follow-up survey, leaving a total of 337 who provided data for the telephone survey.

At its peak, 199 of the soldiers, according to the unit roster, were married to spouses who could have participated in the study. As of January 1997, 169 of the original spouses were eligible to participate in the survey. Seventy-two of these spouses responded to the telephone survey. Of 31 new marriages since the deployment, 24 spouses responded to the survey, for a total of 96. In addition, 6 engaged partners of the 11 couples who had been engaged to each other since fall 1994 participated in the telephone survey for a total of 102 respondents. Spouses and engaged partners were surveyed about their attitudes and opinions about the deployment and given an eight-item organizational commitment scale similar to the short form given to the soldiers but with appropriate wording changes in the CC items. The AC items were the same as for the soldiers. The revised CC items were as follows: (a) It would be too costly for my spouse or fiancée to leave the military in the near future; (b) I am afraid of what might happen if my spouse or fiancée quit the military without having another job lined up; (c) a large part of my life would be disrupted if my spouse or fiancée decided to leave the military now; and (d) one of the problems with my spouse or fiancée leaving the military would be the lack of available alternatives.

Sample Survey of Military Personnel Sample and Materials

The Sample Survey of Military Personnel (SSMP) is administered twice a year, in the spring and fall, to a sample of Army personnel in grades from private through colonel by the Army Personnel Survey Office at the U.S. Army Research Institute. Although general demographic information and general satisfaction items are used in each survey, other topics vary depending on the interests of various Army agencies that sponsor the unique questions used in each survey. The SSMP is sent by mail to soldiers in Europe and sent to personnel support centers at other locations around the world for direct distribution to soldiers through Army channels. Overall, approximately 10% of active Army officers and about 2% of the active Army enlisted soldiers are sampled in each survey. In the fall 1997 SSMP (SSMP 97),

3,948 officers (4.9% of officers) and 4,044 enlisted soldiers (1.1% of enlisted soldiers) responded to the survey for a total of 7,992 respondents. Although the Army Personnel Survey Office has not been able to determine the actual response rate for each survey, the office estimates that the actual response rate is approximately 50%. We administered the short, four-item forms of the AC and CC scales developed in the MFO sample to all soldiers in the SSMP 97. As before, all items were rated on a 5-point Likert-type scale, from *strongly agree* to *strongly disagree,* with a midpoint of *neither agree nor disagree.*

RESULTS

Fall 1994 MFO Survey

Because of the potential for differences between RC and active Army soldiers on organizational commitment, discriminant analyses were conducted predicting group—active Army or RC—membership from organizational commitment items in the survey. Both the Box's M test and the canonical discriminant function were significant ($p < .01$). Consequently, we decided to analyze the survey items separately for active Army and RC personnel. However, there were too few cases available for active Army personnel to perform a reliable factor analysis ($n = 91$) for the 15-item set. Therefore, we performed a confirmatory factor analysis (CFA) of the commitment scales for the RC soldier data only ($n = 402$).

The 15 commitment items were subjected to a two-factor CFA using LISREL (Jöreskog & Sörbom, 1993). The model for this 15-item CFA is shown in Figure 1.

The LISREL goodness of fit statistics supported the hypothesized factor structure. The goodness of fit statistics are reported in Table 1. Although the chi-square test result of 324.36 was significant, indicating that the hypothesized model could not completely account for the covariance structure analyzed, this result can be attributed, at least in part, to the large sample size because as sample size increases above 200, the chi-square test becomes very sensitive. The goodness of fit index (GFI) of .92 and the Root Mean Square Residual of .058 indicated that the correlation matrix is fairly well reproduced using the hypothesized path diagram and factor loadings. The more conservative adjusted goodness of fit index (AGFI) is slightly smaller at .89 but still close to the .90 level. The correlation between the latent AC and CC constructs was .23, indicating some overlap between these constructs. Cronbach's (1951) alpha for the AC scale was .75 and .88 for the CC scale. The AC scale alpha was below the reported median alpha of .85 for this scale, and the CC scale alpha was somewhat above the typical .79 for this scale (Meyer & Allen, 1997, p. 120). A shortened form of each of these scales was formed for use in later research by selecting the four items from each scale with the highest factor loadings.

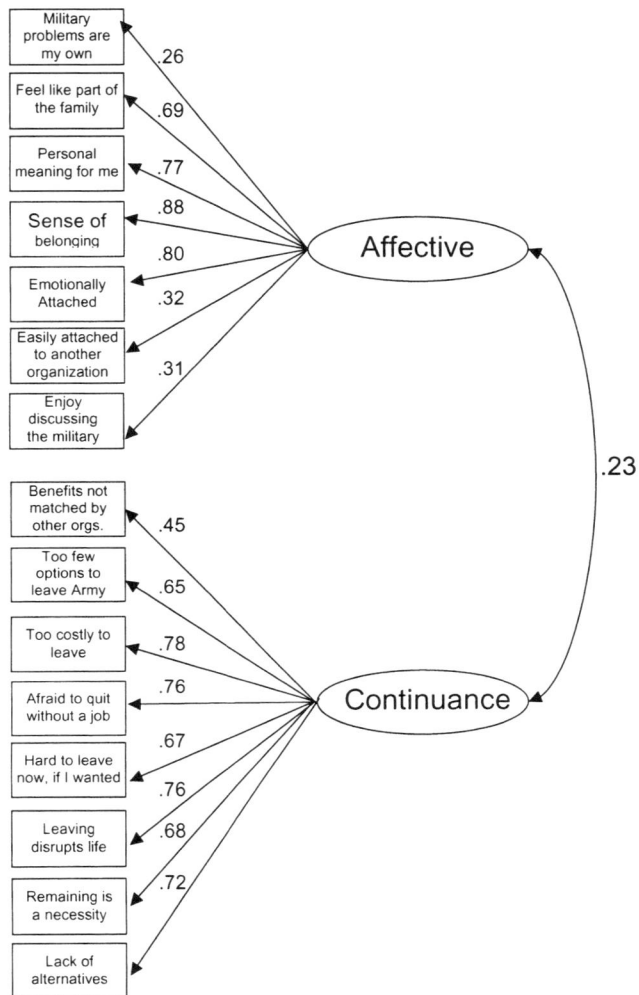

FIGURE 1. MFO 94 confirmed path diagram and factor loadings for affective and continuance commitment items.

Spring 1995 MFO Survey

To assess the impact of organizational commitment on performance, we used the organizational commitment scores on the fall 1994 survey to divide the RC soldiers in that survey into high and low commitment groups on the AC and CC scales. Data from a total of 211 RC soldiers were available for these analyses. We then used AC and CC as independent variables with these commitment groupings of high and low forming the two levels of each variable. The following four groups were formed: High Affective Commitment and Low Continuance Commitment (HALC, $n = 45$), High Affective Commitment and High Continuance Commitment (HAHC, $n = 65$), Low Affective Commitment and Low Continuance Commitment (LALC, $n = 61$), and Low Affective and High Continuance Commitment (LAHC, $n = 40$). We then performed a 2×2 factorial analysis of variance (ANOVA) on the scores each participant earned on each of two job knowledge tests. We used SPSS 10.0 for Windows for these and all subsequent ANOVAs and regression analyses (SPSS, 1999). Each score for both the MFO Job Knowledge test and the General Soldiering Job Knowledge test was recorded as percentage correct. Meyer and Allen's (1997) theory predicted that AC should positively influence performance, whereas CC should negatively affect performance or perhaps have no effect on performance at all. Based on our review of previous research, we expected that the HALC group would perform best on both tests, whereas those in the LAHC group would perform the worst. Those in the other two groups would probably fall somewhere in between the HALC and LAHC groups in performance. This means that we expected a significant main effect for AC for each of the job knowledge variables and a significant main effect for CC as well. However, some researchers have indicated that CC may not have any effect on performance (e.g., Angle & Lawson, 1994), in which case there may not be a significant main effect for CC.

Although we expected CC to negatively affect performance, we had no reason to expect these effects to be anything but additive with respect to AC. Therefore, we expected no significant interaction between AC and CC on either of the outcome variables.

The results of both ANOVAs confirmed our predicted results. The main effect for AC was significant for the MFO-specific job knowledge test, $F(1, 207) = 5.71$, $p < .02$, and marginally significant for the General Soldiering Job Knowledge test, $F(1, 207) = 3.57$, $p = .06$. The main effect for CC was significant for the MFO test, $F(1, 207) = 13.74$, $p < .001$, and for the General Soldiering test, $F(1, 207) = 8.92$, $p < .003$. The interactions between AC and CC were nonsignificant for both job knowledge tests. Figure 2 shows that for both performance tests the HALC group performed best and the LAHC group performed the worst.

To assess the combined AC and CC effects, we used Tukey's honestly significant difference (HSD) test to evaluate the differences between pairwise group test performance means. The mean difference required for significance for the MFO scores and for the General Soldiering scores was 10.5% and 11%, respectively ($\alpha = .01$). For both the MFO and General Soldiering scores, this analysis showed that only the HALC and LAHC group means were significantly different from each other. To assess the strength of the effect of AC and CC on performance, we performed a multiple-regression analysis on both the MFO-specific job knowledge test and the General Soldiering test data sets. These analyses showed that AC and CC had a moderate

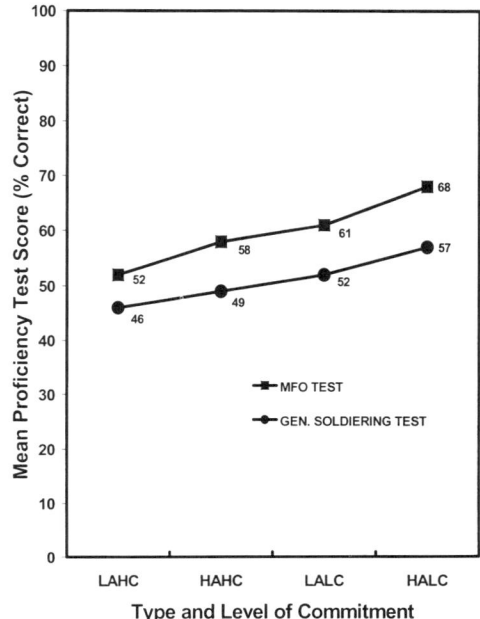

FIGURE 2. Mean MFO specific skills and general soldiering skills test scores as a function of type and level of organizational commitment.

combined effect on MFO test performance, R^2 (adjusted) = .112, and on General Soldiering test performance, R^2 (adjusted) = .107.

These results clearly show that AC and CC, as measured in the fall of 1994, had differential, additive effects on job knowledge performance the following spring, AC having a positive effect and CC having a negative effect on performance. This is consistent with and amplified by the findings of Tisak and Tisak (2000), who found AC and CC to have *traitlike* characteristics that persisted over a 3-year time span as well as *statelike* characteristics that varied between time periods. The results of Tisak and Tisak's study suggest that the influence of AC and CC on subsequent performance is exerted through the traitlike attribute of these constructs.

SSMP 97

Based on the results from the CFA of the fall 1994 MFO data, a two-factor model of organizational commitment was hypothesized and tested with a CFA. The input data for the CFA was a correlation matrix based on the items from the shortened form of the AC and CC scales developed from the 1994 MFO data and administered on the SSMP 97. These correlations were computed from a sample of 7,955 active Army soldiers who responded to the Fall 1997 Sample Survey of Military Personnel (SSMP 97). The LISREL goodness of fit statistics supported the hypothesized factor structure. Due to the large sample size ($n = 7,955$) the chi-square test result was significant, indicating that the hypothesized model could not completely account for the covariance structure analyzed. As in the earlier fall 1994 MFO analyses, the significant chi-square test result can be attributed principally to a very large sample size ($n = 7,955$). The other goodness of fit statistics were more supportive of the CFA results. The GFI of .97 and the Root Mean Square Residual of .040 indicate that the correlation matrix is adequately reproduced using the hypothesized path diagram and factor loadings. The GFI of .97 fits the data very well. The goodness of fit statistics are reported in Table 1. The AGFI is slightly more conservative at .95. The correlation between the Affective latent construct and Continuance is .38, indicating a fair degree of overlap between these constructs. The coefficient alpha for the Affective scale was .89 and .86 for the Continuance scale. The path diagram for these results is shown in Figure 3.

Because the SSMP asks a variety of questions about soldier attitudes and career intentions, we were able to examine the relation between AC and CC and self-reported measures of retention intention, readiness, and well-being. Based on Meyer and Allen's theory (Meyer & Allen, 1997) we predicted that retention intentions should be positively affected by both AC and CC and that the highest retention intentions would be found among those in the HAHC group, whereas those in the LALC group should have the lowest retention intentions. As in the MFO spring 1995 analyses, we split both AC and CC dimensions at the median scores as measured on the SSMP 97. This resulted in the same four groupings with the following cell sizes: HALC, 1,412; HAHC, 2,427; LALC, 2,040; and LAHC, 1,889. We asked soldiers to indicate their retention intentions on the following 6-point scale: "Definitely leave on completion of my present obligation"; "probably leave on completion of my present obligation"; "probably stay in beyond my present obligation, but not necessarily to retirement"; "definitely stay in beyond my present obligation, but not necessarily to retirement"; "probably stay in until retirement"; and "definitely stay in until retire-

TABLE 1
Confirmatory Factor Analyses Goodness-of-fit Statistics

Statistic	SSMP 97	MFO Samples		
		Soldier 94	Soldier 97	Spouse 97
χ^2	826.20	324.36	37.10	42.10
df	19.00	89.00	19.00	19.00
p	0.00	0.00	0.01	0.01
GFI	0.97	0.92	0.97	0.91
AGFI	0.95	0.89	0.94	0.83
RMS Residual	0.040	0.058	0.049	0.047
n	7,955.00	402.00	289.00	90.00

Notes. GFI = goodness of fit index; AGFI = adjusted goodness of fit index; RMS = Root Mean Square.

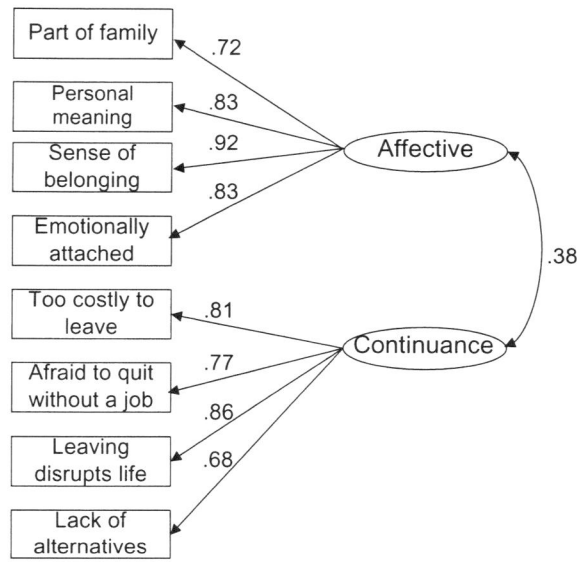

FIGURE 3. SSMP 97 confirmed path diagram and factor loadings for affective and continuance commitment items.

ment." Reenlistment intentions measured with a single-item scale such as ours historically have had strong predictive validity. For example, Hom and Hulin (1981), using a 7-point scale ranging from *unlikely* to *likely,* found that reenlistment intention correlated ($r = .70$) with actual reenlistment behavior 6 months later. Using a similar measure, Motowidlo and Lawton (1984) showed that retention intentions measured 6 months prior to the decision point correlated ($r = .66$) with the actual retention decisions.

As predicted, soldiers in the HAHC group were more likely to say they would stay in the Army longer than were soldiers in any of the other three groups. And, also as predicted, soldiers in the LALC group were more likely to say they would leave the Army. These results are depicted in Figure 4 along with all four group means.

The main effect for AC was significant, $F(1, 7764) = 1632.066, p < .001$, as was the main effect for CC, $F(1, 7764) = 173.858, p < .001$. The interaction was also significant, $F(1, 7764) = 74.879, p < .001$. We used Tukey's HSD test to evaluate the interaction simple effects. The difference between pairwise group means required for significance set at $\alpha = .01$ was 0.167. The difference interval of ± 0.167 is shown around each of the group means in Figure 4. This analysis showed that all pairwise comparisons for the four group means were significant except for the differences between the HALC and HAHC groups. Clearly, low CC had a bigger neg-

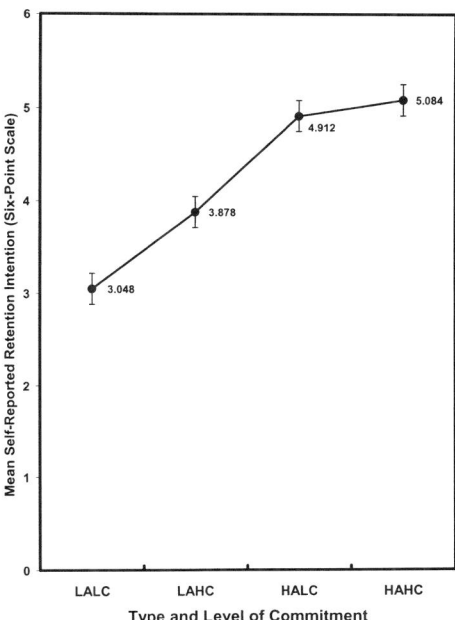

FIGURE 4. Mean SSMP 97 retention intention scores as a function of type and level of organizational commitment.

ative effect associated with retention intentions at the low level of AC. Multiple-regression analysis showed that AC, CC, and their interaction had a fairly strong combined effect on self-reported retention intention, R^2(adjusted) = .208.

We also asked these soldiers to indicate their readiness to perform their wartime duties on a 5-point Likert-type scale ranging from *not at all prepared* to *very well prepared,* with *moderately prepared* as a midpoint. As shown in Figure 5, we found that the HALC group was significantly more likely to say they were prepared to perform their mission than any of the other groups, whereas those in the LAHC group were more likely to say they were less prepared. Both the main effects for AC and CC were significant, $F(1, 7814) = 620.032, p < .001$, and $F(1, 7814) = 11.607, p < .001$, respectively, as was the interaction effect, $F(1, 7814) = 8.165, p < .004$). Again, we used Tukey's HSD test to evaluate the interaction simple effects. The difference between pairwise group means required for significance set at $\alpha = .01$ was 0.073. The difference interval of ± 0.073 is shown around each of the group means in Figure 5. This analysis showed that all pairwise comparisons for the four group means were significant except for the differences between the LALC and LAHC groups. The significant interaction effect showed that AC had a fairly strong relation to readiness, but the effect was more pronounced at the low level of CC. A multiple-regression analysis showed that the strength of effect of the combined commitment variables and their interaction on self-assessed readiness was weak to moderately strong, R^2(adjusted) = .073. These findings, although

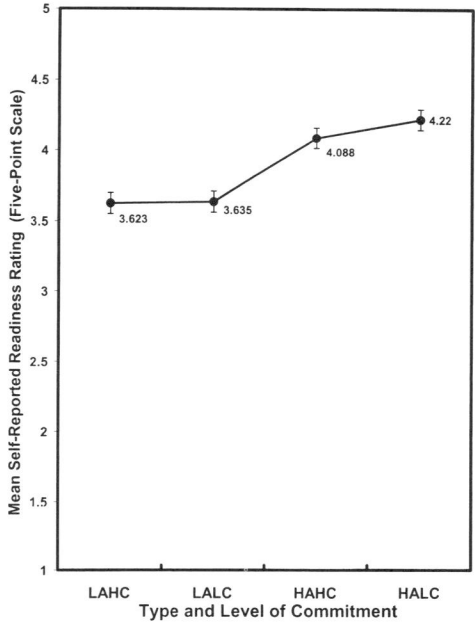

FIGURE 5. Mean SSMP 97 self-reported readiness ratings as a function of type and level of organizational commitment.

less interesting than our earlier findings from the MFO soldier performance data, are consistent with the Meyer and Allen theory of the effect of organizational commitment on performance in that CC may have negative effects on performance or no effect at all, whereas AC will always have a positive effect on performance. Of course, self-assessed readiness is a far different measure of performance from the knowledge tests administered to the MFO soldiers and may in part explain the differences in results.

As an index of soldier well-being, we examined the soldiers' responses to the SSMP that asked them to report their level of morale on a 5-point Likert-type scale ranging from *very low* to *very high* with *moderate* as a midpoint. As Figure 6 shows, we found that the HALC group had a higher mean morale score than any of the other groups, but not much different from the other high AC group.

Both low AC groups had about the same mean morale scores at each level of CC. These descriptive results were confirmed by the ANOVA results in that the main effect for AC was significant, $F(1, 7815) = 1136.881, p < .001$, whereas the main effect for CC was not, $F(1, 7815) = 2.293, p = .13$. However, the interaction between AC and CC was significant, $F(1, 7815) = 24.205, p < .001$. Once again we used Tukey's HSD test to evaluate the interaction simple effects. The difference between pairwise group means required for significance set at $\alpha = .01$ was 0.131. The difference interval of ± 0.131 is shown around each of the group means in Figure 6. This analysis showed that all pairwise comparisons for the four group means

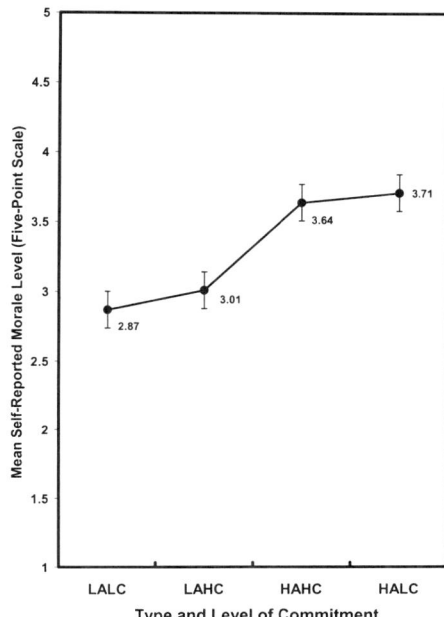

FIGURE 6. Mean SSMP 97 self-reported morale ratings as a function of type and level of organizational commitment.

were significant except for the differences between the HALC and HAHC groups. These results indicated that AC was more strongly related to well-being, at least as measured here, than was CC. The interaction was due to a small but significant difference between low and high CC groups only at the low level of AC. The results for the self-reported morale ratings look very similar to those for the self-assessed readiness ratings, in that AC seems to have had a strong effect and CC a relatively weak one. Multiple-regression analysis showed that the combined effect of the commitment variables and their interaction was moderately related to well-being, at least as measured here, R^2 (adjusted) = .13.

January 1997 MFO Survey

We conducted two CFAs on the data collected from the MFO 1997 telephone survey of mostly RC soldiers and their spouses. A separate CFA was done for RC soldiers and spouses using the model specified in the CFA performed on the fall 1997 SSMP data. The model shown in Figure 7 is based on the matrix of intercorrelations for 289 soldiers.

The CFA results for the spouses are shown in Figure 8. It should be noted that the spouse CFA is based on only 90 cases. Table 1 contains the goodness of fit statistics for the two MFO models as well as the SSMP 97 model. Because both CFAs have GFIs greater than .90, we concluded that the proposed factor struc-

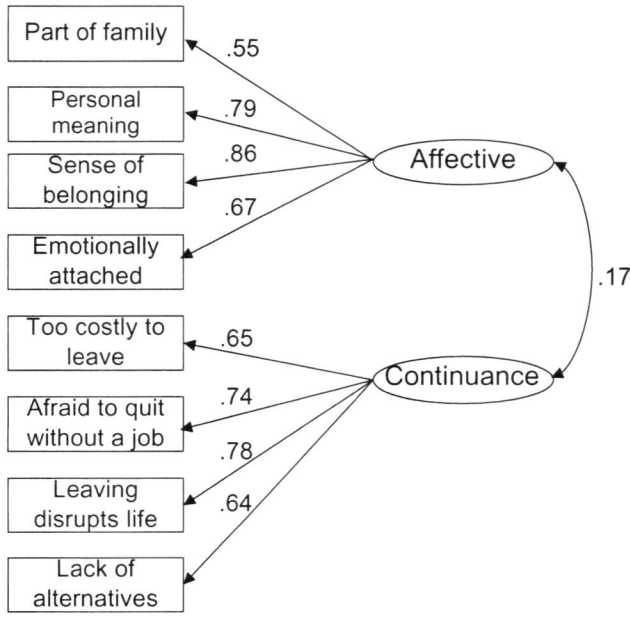

FIGURE 7. MFO 97 reserve component soldier telephone survey confirmed path diagram and factor loadings for affective and continuance commitment items.

tures and path diagrams closely fit their data. Further, this factor structure holds for different samples and genders. However, because the adjusted GFI falls below .90 for spouses, the fit of the data for the spouse model with an AGFI of .83 is marginal. Undoubtedly the small sample size, $n = 90$, was a factor in these results. The coefficient alpha for the soldier Affective scale was .81 and .87 for spouses. The coefficient alpha for the soldier Continuance scale was .78 for soldiers and .86 for spouses. Note that the AC and CC constructs are a bit more correlated (.38) in the spouse sample than in the soldier sample (.17). We also correlated the spouse AC and CC scale scores with the corresponding soldier scores related to them. The correlation coefficient for the relationship between soldiers and their spouses or fiancées was small but significant for the spouse or fiancée AC–soldier AC scales and for the spouse or fiancée CC–soldier CC scales, ($n = 87$) $= .26$, $p < .05$, in both cases. Neither the spouse or fiancée AC–soldier CC nor the soldier AC–spouse or fiancée CC correlation coefficient was significant. Although the sample is small, we are encouraged that the spouse model so closely resembles the soldier model even though we asked slightly different CC questions of the spouses.

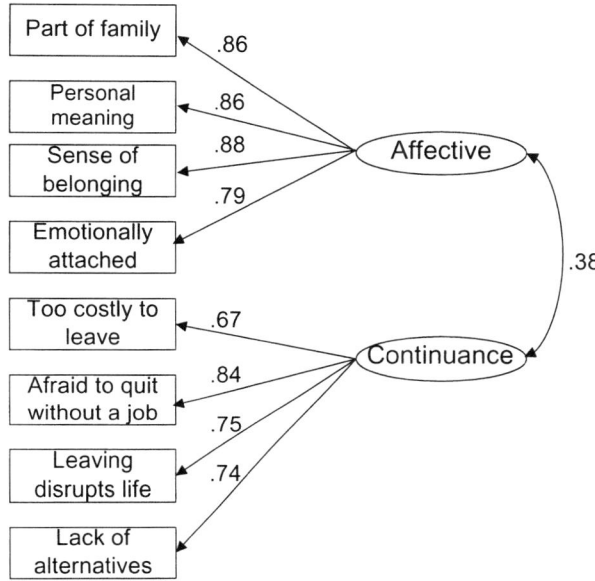

FIGURE 8. MFO 97 reserve component spouse telephone survey confirmed path diagram and factor loadings for affective and continuance commitment items.

DISCUSSION

We set out to accomplish three goals with this research. The first two goals were to assess the factor structure and reliability of affective and continuance organizational commitment scales in a variety of military settings and to develop shorter scales that military researchers easily could use on a variety of military questionnaires. The expected factor structure of the AC and CC scales was confirmed in our initial 1994 investigation with the MFO soldiers. Using the data from this 1994 study, we then were able to develop a four-item scale for AC and a four-item scale for CC that proved to be highly reliable. In general, the scales of AC and CC, especially the abbreviated versions, appear suitable for use with military samples of both soldiers and their spouses and can be given over the telephone as well as in written questionnaires.

Having accomplished our first two objectives, our third goal was to demonstrate the utility of our AC and CC measures for predicting outcomes important to the Army. Our results showed that organizational commitment theory as put forward by Meyer and Allen (1997) worked rather well in predicting important behavioral outcomes, at least for AC and CC. These results were consistent with those of

Karrasch (2003/this issue) in that they demonstrated that one must know about both types of commitment to accurately predict results for a variety of these outcomes. We believe that the MFO results demonstrating a relation between organizational commitment measured in the fall of 1994 and subsequent performance measured in the spring of 1995 are particularly important because they offer strong evidence for a causal link between commitment and performance. Furthermore, based on our results and those of Tisak and Tisak (2000), we propose that the mechanism for the influence of organizational commitment on subsequent performance rests largely in the traitlike attributes of both AC and CC.

The abbreviated commitment measures developed here offer the military a simple but powerful way to track these important motivational precursors of soldier performance, retention, and well-being. With further development and standardization, these measures of AC and CC may well function together as predictors of individual service member willingness to remain in the service, perform well, and be a good citizen. Collectively these measures may well serve as leading indicators of military readiness.

ACKNOWLEDGMENTS

Ronald B. Tiggle is now at the Division of Health Care Statistics, National Center for Health Statistics.

The views, opinions, and/or findings contained in this article are solely those of the authors and should not be construed as an official Department of the Army or DOD position, policy, or decision, unless so designated by other documentation.

REFERENCES

Allen, N. J., & Meyer, J. P. (1990). The measurement and antecedents of affective, continuance, and normative commitment to the organization. *Journal of Occupational Psychology, 63,* 1–18.

Angle, H. L., & Lawson, M. B. (1994). Organizational commitment and employees' performance ratings: Both type of commitment and type of performance count. *Psychological Reports, 75,* 1539–1551.

Brown, R. B. (1996). Organizational commitment: Clarifying the concept and simplifying the existing construct typology. *Journal of Vocational Behavior, 49,* 230–251.

Cronbach, L. J., Jr. (1951). Coefficient alpha and the internal structure of tests. *Psychometrika, 16,* 297–334.

Dunham, R. B., Grube, J. A., & Castaneda, M. B. (1994). Organizational commitment: The utility of an integrative definition. *Journal of Applied Psychology, 79,* 370–380.

Hackett, R. D., Bycio, P., & Hausdorf, P. A. (1994). Further assessment of Meyer and Allen's (1991) three-component model of organizational commitment. *Journal of Applied Psychology, 79,* 15–23.

Hom, P. W., & Hulin, C. L. (1981). A competitive test of the prediction of reenlistment by several models. *Journal of Applied Psychology, 66,* 23–39.

Jöreskog, K. G., & Sörbom, D. (1993). *LISREL 8: Structural equation modeling with the SIMPLIS command language.* Hillsdale, NJ: Lawrence Erlbaum Associates, Inc.

Karrasch, A. I. (2003/this issue). Antecedents and consequences of organizational commitment. *Military Psychology, 15,* 225–236.

Kim, S., Price, J. L., Mueller, C. W., & Watson, T. W. (1996). The determinants of career intent among physicians at a U.S. Air Force hospital. *Human Relations, 47,* 947–976.

Martin, T. N., & O'Laughlin, M. S. (1984). Predictors of organizational commitment: The study of part-time Army reservists. *Journal of Vocational Behavior, 25,* 270–283.

Mathieu, J. E., & Zajac, D. M. (1990). A review and meta-analysis of the antecedents, correlates, and consequences of organizational commitment. *Psychological Bulletin, 108,* 171–194.

Meyer, J. P., & Allen, N. J. (1984). Testing the "side-bet theory" of organizational commitment: Some methodological considerations. *Journal of Applied Psychology, 69,* 372–378.

Meyer, J. P., & Allen, N. J. (1997). *Commitment in the workplace: Theory, research, and application.* Thousand Oaks, CA: Sage.

Motowidlo, S. J., & Lawton, G. W. (1984). Affective and cognitive factors in soldiers' reenlistment decisions. *Journal of Applied Psychology, 69,* 157–166.

Oliver, L. W., Tiggle, R. B., & Hayes, S. M. (1996). *Preliminary report on selected life course variables and reasons for volunteering for the 28th Sinai deployment.* (Tech. Rep. No. 1046). Alexandria, VA: U.S. Army Research Institute for the Behavioral and Social Sciences.

Phelps, R. H., & Farr, B. J. (Eds.). (1996). *Reserve component soldiers as peacekeepers.* Alexandria, VA: U.S. Army Research Institute for the Behavioral and Social Sciences. (DTIC No. AD–A321 857)

Porter, L., & Smith, F. (1970). *The etiology of organizational commitment: A longitudinal study of the initial stages of employee-organization reactions.* Unpublished manuscript, University of California-Irvine.

Reynolds, D. H. & Campbell, R. C. (1996). Development and administration of measures: Sinai peacekeeping performance. In R. H Phelps & B. J. Farr (Eds.), *Reserve component soldiers as peacekeepers* (pp. 119–162). Alexandria, VA: U.S. Army Research Institute for the Behavioral and Social Sciences. (DTIC No. AD–A321 857)

Rosen, L. N., & Martin, L. (1996). Childhood antecedents of psychological adaptation to military life. *Military Medicine: An International Journal, 161,* 665–668.

Segal, D. R., & Tiggle, R. B. (1997). Attitudes of citizen-soldiers toward military missions in the post-cold war world. *Armed Forces and Society, 23,* 373–390.

SPSS (1999). *SPSS Base 10.0 User's Guide.* Chicago: Author.

Teplitzky, M. L. (1991). *Junior Army officer retention intentions: A path analytic model.* (Tech. Rep. No. 934). Alexandria, VA: U. S. Army Research Institute for the Behavioral and Social Sciences. (DTIC No. AD–A242 094)

Tisak, J., & Tisak, M. S. (2000). Permanency and ephemerality of psychological measures with application to organizational commitment. *Psychological Methods, 5,* 175–198.

MILITARY PSYCHOLOGY, 2003, *15*(3), 209–224

Commitment to Nested Collectives in Special Operations Forces

Tonia S. Heffner and Paul A. Gade
U.S. Army Research Institute

Contemporary investigations of workplace commitment include research on commitment components and commitment to multiple, and sometimes nested, work units. Research on commitment within the hierarchical military structure may be particularly reflective of these perspectives. Affective commitment to 2 nested organizational units (Special Operations Forces and the military) was hypothesized to be distinguishable from each another and from military continuance commitment. Further, a model portraying the hypothesized relations between satisfaction and affective commitment for the 2 organizational units and career intentions was examined. Special Operations personnel (*n* = 3,968) from 3 service branches completed satisfaction and career intentions items in addition to modified versions (Gade, Tiggle, & Schumm, 2003/this issue) of the Meyer and Allen (1984) commitment scales. Results of the research supported the distinction between the commitment scales and provided support for the model. Implications for operational environments and future research are discussed.

Research on organizational commitment has demonstrated relations with a myriad of organizationally valued outcomes, including job performance, organizational citizenship behaviors, absenteeism, and turnover (Becker, Billings, Eveleth, & Gilbert, 1996; Mathieu & Zajac, 1990). Military researchers long have been interested in organizational commitment and the application of commitment research findings to the operational environment because of the importance of these outcomes to national defense (cf. Sterling & Allen, 1983). For example, military researchers have a strong interest in the relation between organizational commitment and turnover intentions, particularly when economic and societal conditions give rise to decreased enlistments and increased attrition.

Requests for reprints should be sent to Tonia S. Heffner, U.S. Army Research Institute, TAPC-ARI-RS, 5001 Eisenhower Ave., Alexandria, VA 22333-5600. E-mail: heffnert@ari.army.mil

Researchers have determined commitment is not a single entity (McGee & Ford, 1987; Meyer & Allen, 1984, 1997); rather, it has multiple components, including affective (AC) and continuance commitment (CC). To examine commitment in the military thoroughly, it is important to consider the possible impact of commitment components to more than one work unit (Reichers, 1985) on organizational outcomes. The purpose of this research was to examine the relations of commitment components with other organizationally valued constructs. Initially, we tested our assumption that commitment to nested military units has meaning for military service members, can be assessed using commitment measures derived from Meyer and Allen (1997), and can be distinguished from commitment to the larger organization psychometrically (Becker, 1992; Heffner & Rentsch, 2001). Second, we used a model derived from Mueller and Lawler's (1999) nested collectives theory of commitment to explore some of the potential antecedents of organizational commitment. In this model, satisfaction with organizational collectives influences AC to those collectives, and these work attitudes influence career intentions, a valued outcome in the military context. To achieve these purposes, a brief review of multiple-constituencies commitment research and Mueller and Lawler's model of nested collectives are presented. Building from these bases, we present a nested collectives model of work attitudes, a model we empirically tested with Special Operations Forces personnel. Finally, the findings are interpreted and discussed for operational environments and as a launching point for future research.

COMMITMENT IN ORGANIZATIONS

Research on work commitments currently reflects Meyer and Allen's (1991) three-component model of commitment, including CC, AC, and normative commitment (NC). Commitment toward conceptually distinct foci, such as the organization, occupation, or union (Barling & Wade, 1990; Mathieu & Zajac, 1990; Vandenberg & Scarpello, 1994) is assessed using this model. Reichers (1985, 1986) theorized and tested the idea that employees might form commitments to one or more organizationally relevant groups (i.e., nested) in addition to the organization. Conducted prior to the introduction of the three-component model, Reichers' work reflects the previously dominant view of organizational commitment as wholly affective. Contemporary research on multiple commitments has continued to center on AC. Becker (1992) and Becker et al. (1996) demonstrated that employees do develop AC to multiple organizational entities, including the supervisor, top management, and the organization. Further support is provided by Ellermers, de Gilder, and van den Heuvel (1998), who found team and organizational commitment are distinguishable constructs with different patterns of relations to "work-related variables" (p. 722) despite a high correlation ($r = .61$) between the commitment variables.

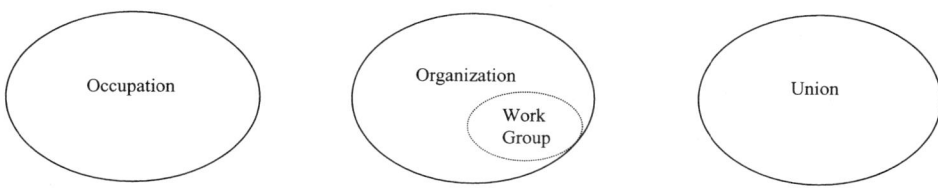

FIGURE 1. The solid lines indicate independent commitment collectives. The dashed lines indicate a nested commitment collective.

This research provided the foundation for further exploration of the possible foci of AC and the possibility of multiple CCs and NCs. Reichers and Becker and his colleagues (Becker, 1992; Becker et al., 1996; Reichers, 1985, 1986) presented and empirically supported a conceptualization of AC to multiple foci that are distinct from one another (e.g., supervisor, organization). One implicit assumption is that commitments to multiple foci are independent of one another. Will commitment to multiple foci exist if the foci are interdependent (i.e., nested)? Although Reichers and Becker examined structurally nested foci (e.g., organization, top managers, and coworkers), they were conceptualized and tested as independent constructs.

COMMITMENT TO NESTED ORGANIZATIONAL COLLECTIVES

Lawler (1992) and Mueller and Lawler (1999) presented a theory and model of commitment in organizations that specifically addresses nested organizational constituencies. Similar to the propositions of Reichers and Becker (Becker, 1992; Becker et al., 1996; Reichers 1985, 1986), Lawler postulated that employees develop AC to multiple organizational foci. These foci, however, can be conceptually distinct as proposed by Reichers and Becker, or can be nested. Nested organizational entities are those in which a larger group encompasses a smaller one. For example, within an organization, the department subsumes the work group or the military subsumes Special Operations Forces (see Figure 1).

A further proposition that makes nested commitment collectives particularly intriguing and distinct from independent commitment entities is that employees "form different degrees of attachment to the multiple, nested collectives" (Lawler, 1992, p. 334). Face-to-face interaction between organizational employees contributes to the degree of attachments to proximal and distal collectives. Therefore, employees should have more face-to-face interaction in—and thus greater commitment to—the smaller, more proximal organizational unit than to the larger, more distal organizational unit.

Mueller and Lawler (1999) found some support for this hypothesis from schoolteachers who reported higher AC to the school than to the school system. Likewise, within a military context, Diana (1998) found Army Special Forces soldiers reported highest AC to their 10- to 12-person team, lowest to the Army, with Special Forces—a sub unit of the Army composed of many teams and other levels of organization—falling in between. The team and Army AC scales showed low intercorrelations and differential relations with variables such as perceived support and propensity to remain in the Army.

Other researchers have provided support for Lawler's (1992) model. Hunt and Morgan (1994) reexamined Becker's (1992) data to investigate whether the organization was just one of multiple commitment constituencies or if commitment to the organization was a key mediating variable between "lower" commitments and organizational outcomes. Consistent with nested commitment theory, Hunt and Morgan found that constituency-specific ACs contribute to global organizational commitment and that the relation between constituency-specific AC and organizational outcomes is mediated by global AC. Heffner and Rentsch (2001) tested a nested model of AC and social interaction in the work group, department, and overall organization. Consistent with Lawler's propositions, employees reported the highest commitment to the most proximal constituency, the work group, and the lowest commitment to the most distal constituency, the overall organization. The degree of social interaction in each constituency predicted the degree of AC to that constituency. Further, the relation between work-group AC and organizational AC was fully mediated by department AC. In other words, both AC and social interaction decreased as the psychological distance within the organization increased, and AC to proximal organizational entities predicted AC to distal entities within the organization.

The extant literature on organizational commitment provides a strong foundation for the existence of multiple components of commitment. Furthermore, the previously mentioned research provides some evidence to support AC to multiple foci and the mediating role between proximal commitment constituencies, distal commitment constituencies, and organizational outcomes.

A MODEL OF SATISFACTION, COMMITMENT, AND CAREER INTENTIONS FOR MULTIPLE FOCI

An abundance of research has examined the relation between organizational commitment, particularly AC, and job satisfaction. This research has generally established job satisfaction as a precursor to AC (Lease, 1998; Mathieu & Zajac, 1990). Job satisfaction is often defined globally to include such factors as satisfaction with leadership and other workplace factors (Lease, 1998; Spector, 1997). A second well-established relation is a causal link between AC, CC, and NC and turnover/career intentions—the intention to voluntarily leave the organization (Angle & Perry, 1981; Mathieu & Zajac, 1990; Porter, Steers, Mowday, & Boulian, 1974).

Consistent with the extant literature, Mueller and Lawler (1999) hypothesized that job satisfaction will influence commitment. Specifically, job satisfaction will directly influence AC to the proximal collective (cf. Rusbult & Farrell, 1983), indirectly influence AC to the distal collective through the proximal collective, and may directly influence AC to the distal collective. "Because the more proximate unit will always possess an 'interaction advantage' … [interactions] will affect commitment to the local unit (through job satisfaction) more strongly than commitment to a more distant unit" (Mueller & Lawler, 1999, p. 329).

The commitment to nested collectives model is at the individual level of analysis. Even though participants report on multiple organizational levels, no aggregated variables exist. Nevertheless, an important lesson from multilevel theory must be applied to nested collectives theory. According to Schneider (1985) and Ostroff (1993), relations between constructs that exist at one level may or may not be paralleled at another level of analysis. Like multilevel models, we cannot simply assume a relation between constructs for one organizational entity exists for a different organizational entity.

Combining nested collectives theory with the traditional relations between job satisfaction, commitment, and career intentions and a multilevel approach suggests the relations should be tested for other organizational collectives. The Mueller and Lawler (1999) model addresses commitment to multiple organizational collectives, but just as commitment to multiple foci exists in organization, so might other work attitudes. Examining schoolteachers and Air Force medical personnel, Mueller and Lawler (1999) discovered job satisfaction directly influenced commitment to the proximal constituency (i.e., the school and medical center) and directly and indirectly influenced commitment to the distal constituency (i.e., the school system and Air Force). Another way of conceptualizing this relation is that satisfaction with a particular collective is a strong predictor of AC to that collective. According to Mueller and Lawler (1999), commitment to a proximal constituency will influence commitment to a distal constituency. Likewise, satisfaction with a distal constituency is likely to influence satisfaction to a proximal constituency. Regardless of the multiple constituencies within the organization, the outcome variable of interest is turnover/career intentions. Although turnover/career intentions toward a distal collective have importance for the individual and his or her direct colleagues, organizational interests lie in intentions toward the organization. For that reason, the ultimate outcome of the model is organizational career intentions.

FIGURE 2. Hypothesized Model of Nested Satisfaction and Commitment.

HYPOTHESES AND MODEL

We needed to establish that service members could discriminate commitment to nested military constituencies before testing the Mueller and Lawler (1999) model. Furthermore, we needed to discover if commitment to various organizational constituencies could be assessed using similar measures of commitment and, finally, if commitment to organizational constituencies could be distinguished psychometrically (Becker, 1992; Heffner & Rentsch, 2001).

Hypothesis 1: Three distinct factors of commitment representing Special Forces AC, military AC, and military CC will be discernible from the data.

After making the distinction between components and foci of commitment, the model of work attitudes to nested collectives can be tested. The model (see Figure 2) is an extension and refinement of previous research on organizational commitment (Diana, 1998; Heffner & Rentsch, 2001; Mueller & Lawler, 1999) summarized by the following hypotheses.

Hypothesis 2: Satisfaction with Special Operations will influence Special Operations AC.

Hypothesis 3: Satisfaction with Special Operations will influence satisfaction with the military.

Hypothesis 4: Satisfaction with the military will influence military AC.

Hypothesis 5: Special Operations AC will influence military AC.

Hypothesis 6: Military AC will influence career intentions.

METHOD

Participants

Responses from 3,968 enlisted personnel (76%) and officers of the Special Operations Forces were examined. The participants were 2,869 Army, 454 Navy, and 640 Air Force service members serving in the joint-service Special Operations Command. The remaining 5 participants did not report service branch. The respondents were all men with a mean of 13.3 years in military service and 8.3 years in Special Operations. Eighty-nine percent of the sample was married.

Measures

A 118-item survey was developed to assess the impact of personnel tempo (PERSTEMPO), defined as the frequency of deployments and other time-dependent activities on personnel attitudes. Our research focused only on six self-report measures in the survey. These were military CC, military AC, Special Operations AC, satisfaction with the military, satisfaction with Special Operations, and career intentions. (For a fuller description of this survey and its development, see Human Resources Research Organization, 1998.)

Military continuance commitment.   A shortened version of the Meyer and Allen (1984) eight-item Continuance Commitment Scale was used to assess military CC. Previous work by Gade, Tiggle, & Schumm (2003/this issue) demonstrated that this four-item CC scale, with two lack-of-alternatives items and two high-sacrifice items, was a comprehensive representation of the construct (see Table 1 for the items used). As in previous research, the items were positively worded and rated on a 5-point Likert-type scale ranging from 1 (*strongly disagree*) to 5 (*strongly agree*). The coefficient alpha estimate of reliability was .87, which is slightly higher than typically received with the eight-item scale and consistent with the work of Gade et al.

Military affective commitment.   Likewise, a four-item version of the Meyer and Allen (1984) eight-item Affective Commitment Scale, developed by Gade et al. (2003/this issue) was used to assess military AC. The items (see Table 1) were positively worded and rated on a 5-point Likert-type scale ranging from 1(*strongly disagree*) to 5(*strongly agree*). The coefficient alpha estimate of reliability was .88, consistent with the eight-item scale and work of Gade et al.

Special Operations affective commitment.   The four items used to assess military AC were modified to assess Special Operations AC. The items were modified by replacing the word "military" with the words "Special Operations." This type of modification has been supported by previous research (Bishop & Scott, 2000; Diana, 1998; Heffner & Rentsch, 2001). The items (see Table 1) were rated on a 5-point Likert-type scale ranging from 1 (*strongly disagree*) to 5 (*strongly agree*). The coefficient alpha estimate of reliability for this revised scale was .90.

Satisfaction with Special Operations Forces. The satisfaction items were adapted from Diana (1998). Six items were used to measure satisfaction with Special Operations. Sample items include "The frustrations in Special Operations are minor compared to the satisfaction I get from my work" and "All in all, I am really glad I joined Special Operations." The items were rated on a 5-point Likert-type scale ranging from 1 (*strongly disagree*) to 5 (*strongly agree*). The coefficient alpha estimate of reliability was .80.

TABLE 1
Confirmatory Factor Analysis Results for the
Commitment Measures

Scale Items	Factor Loadings		
	1	*2*	*3*
Military Continuance Commitment			
It would be too costly for me to leave the military in the near future.	.80		
I am afraid of what might happen if I quit the military without having another job lined up.	.80		
Too much of my life would be interrupted if I decided to leave the military now.	.85		
One of the problems of leaving the military would be the lack of available alternatives.	.72		
Military Affective Commitment			
I feel like "part of the family" in the military.		.74	
The military has a great deal of personal meaning to me.		.79	
I feel a strong sense of belonging to the military.		.92	
I feel "emotionally attached" to the military.		.82	
Special Operations Affective Commitment			
I feel like "part of the family" in Special Operations.			.78
Special Operations has a great deal of personal meaning to me.			.83
I feel a strong sense of belonging to Special Operations.			.93
I feel "emotionally attached" to Special Operations.			.82

Satisfaction with the military.   The satisfaction with the military items were adapted from Diana (1998) for use in this study. The four items were rated on a 5-point Likert-type scale ranging from 1 (*strongly disagree*) to 5 (*strongly agree*). A sample item is "How satisfied are you with enlisted leadership?" The coefficient alpha estimate of reliability for the satisfaction with the military scale was .80.

Career intentions.   Career intentions is a valuable criterion because it provides information about the soldier's attitude toward military service and provides indications for needed interventions to maintain retention while the opportunity is available to policymakers (Lakhani & Gade, 1992). Career intention is also an accurate indicator of actual turnover behavior. Motowidlo and Lawton (1984) and Johnston (1988) found correlations ranging from .59 to .61 between career intention and actual turnover behavior.

We used a single item to assess career intentions. In response to the question "Which of the following best describes your current career intentions in the service?" participants were asked to choose one of six options ranging from "Definitely stay until retirement" to "Definitely leave after completing my present obligation." See Gade et al. (2003/this issue) for a description of the six response options.

Procedure

Surveys were distributed to participants in the fall of 1997. A study advisory group was established to guide the instrument development and assist in data collection. Typically, survey completion was conducted in a group setting to guarantee maximum efficiency. When all individuals within a component had completed a survey, they were forwarded to the processing center.

RESULTS

Confirmatory Factor Analysis of Commitment Scales

To test Hypothesis 1, the ability of service members to distinguish among military AC, military CC, and Special Operations AC scales, a confirmatory factor analysis (CFA) was performed on the 12 items (see Table 1). The measurement model fit the data well, $\chi^2(51, n = 3,968) = 2245.66, p < .001$, goodness of fit index (GFI) = .91, adjusted goodness of fit index (AGFI) = .88, comparative fit index (CFI) = .93, Tucker–Lewis fit index (TLI) = .91, and root mean square error of approximation (RMSEA) = .10. These fit indexes are recommended on the basis of the sample size and number of parameters estimated (Gerbing & Anderson, 1992; Medsker, Williams, & Holahan, 1994; Pedhazur & Schmelkin, 1991). All items loaded signifi-

TABLE 2
Descriptive Statistics and Correlations for Research Variables

	M	SD	1	2	3	4	5	6
1. Satisfaction with military	3.12	.67	.80					
2. Satisfaction with Special Operations	3.32	.66	.70***	.83				
3. Military continuance commitment	2.93	1.05	.12***	.15***	.87			
4. Military affective commitment	3.14	.88	.52***	.62***	.21***	.89		
5. Special Operations affective commitment	3.66	.92	.42***	.66***	.09***	.53***	.90	
6. Career intentions	4.69[a]	1.81	.19***	.27***	.30***	.35***	.26***	—[b]

Note. $n = 3,968$. Values on the diagonal are coefficient alpha estimates of reliability.
[a]A six point response scale. [b]A single item indicator.
* $p < .05$. ** $p < .01$. *** $p < .001$.

cantly on the intended factor, providing support for Hypothesis 1. The means, standard deviations, coefficient alphas, and correlations for all study variables are presented in Table 2.

Test of the Hypothesized Nested Model

Measurement model.   Figure 2 depicts the hypothesized nested model (Hypotheses 2–5). The nested model incorporated constructs beyond those included in the CFA of the commitment constructs, so a second measurement model was constructed for the 19 items present in the hypothesized nested model. The measurement model fit the data moderately well, χ^2 (143, $n = 3,968$) = 4857.34, $p < .001$, GFI = .87, AGFI = .83, CFI = .90, TLI = .87, and RMSEA = .09. All items loaded significantly on the intended factor.

Hypothesized model.   The nested model was tested using structural equation modeling. The hypothesized model accounted for 47% of the variance in satisfaction with the military, 44% of the variance in Special Operations AC, 39% of the variance in military AC, and 12% of the variance in career intentions. Fit indexes illustrated that the model fit the data well, χ^2 (5, $n = 3,968$) = 349.87, $p < .001$, GFI = .97, AGFI = .91, CFI = .96, TLI = .91, and RMSEA = .13.

Model comparison.   Following the recommendations by Anderson and Gerbing (1988), several nested models were examined using chi-square difference tests to further assess the fit of the model to the data. The difference in the chi-squares between the hypothesized and structurally null models was signifi-

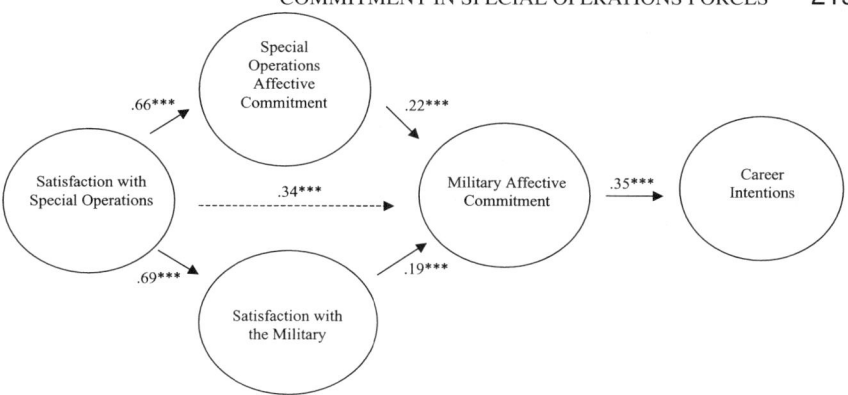

Figure 3. Standardized path estimates for the revised model. Revision indicated by the dashed line.

cant, $\Delta\chi^2$ (5, n = 3,968) = 7293.68, p < .001, which suggests the hypothesized model is a significant improvement in fit over the null model.

Although the hypothesized model provided a good fit to the data, the modification indexes suggested a better fit was possible by adding a direct path from satisfaction with Special Operations Forces to military AC in addition to the hypothesized indirect relation. The revised model accounted for 47% of the variance in satisfaction with the military, 44% of the variance in Special Operations AC, 43% of the variance in military AC, and 12% of the variance in career intentions. Fit indexes indicated that the model fit the data well, χ^2 (4, n = 3,968) = 67.38, p < .001, GFI = .99, AGFI = .97, CFI = .96, TLI = .98, and RMSEA = .06. Furthermore, the difference in the chi-squares was significant, $\Delta\chi^2$ (1, n = 3,968) = 282.49, p < .001, which suggests the revised model is a significant improvement in fit. The standardized path coefficients are presented in Figure 3.

Supporting Hypotheses 2 and 3, the analysis showed that satisfaction with Special Operations Forces was significantly related to both Special Operations AC and satisfaction with the military. As predicted in Hypotheses 4 and 5, the relations of military AC with Special Operations AC and satisfaction with the military were significant. Finally, the significant relation between military AC and career intentions supported Hypothesis 6.

DISCUSSION

Our research had two primary objectives: (a) to assess the distinction between three adapted commitment measures and (b) to develop and test a model of commitment to nested collectives based on Mueller and Lawler's (1999) propositions. The first of these objectives was accomplished by conducting a CFA that supported a distinction between the abbreviated Military Continuance Commitment, Military Affective Commitment, and Special Operations Forces Affective Commitment scales. This finding is notable because it supported the Gade et al. (2003/this issue) conclusion that Meyer and Allen's (1984) AC and CC scales can be condensed without sacrificing the psychometric properties of the scales. To bolster this claim, the reliability and correlation coefficients between the two constructs at the organization level are similar in magnitude to those found in research using the original scales. In further support, these findings were made despite the use of a nontraditional sample of Special Operations Forces personnel.

Additional validity evidence for the abbreviated scales can also be drawn from this study. Not only was the correlation between the condensed scales similar to that obtained with the original scales but also the relations with other constructs exhibited similar patterns. For example, the correlations between military AC and two other constructs, satisfaction with the military and career intentions, are of the same magnitude as typically found in organizational research with the original scales. Likewise, the correlation between military CC and the same two constructs, satisfaction with the military and career intentions, were similar in magnitude to those typically found in organizational research with the original scales. These findings suggest that, in large-scale operational environment data collections where cost and time are limited quantities, the abbreviated scales are reliable and valid measures of AC and CC.

A second important finding from the CFA is the distinction between Special Operations AC and the two military-oriented scales, particularly military AC. Critics have questioned the ability of respondents to make a distinction between the commitment scales when modified to measure commitment to multiple collectives in the same research program. The analyses clearly demonstrate respondents do perceive the constructs as distinct, thus supporting similar previous findings (Bishop & Scott, 2000; Heffner & Rentsch, 2001). The relation between military CC and Special Operations AC is even smaller in magnitude than between military CC and ACs. The relation between military AC and Special Operations AC is moderately high but of the same magnitude as relations between other constructs in this study. This combined evidence suggests it is safe to conclude that the modification of organizational commitment scales to assess commitment to other collectives within an organization is appropriate.

The second objective of this research effort was to test a model of commitment to nested collectives based on Mueller and Lawler's (1999) theory. The analyses support the hypothesized relations between satisfaction and AC to a collective (i.e., Special Operations Forces and the military). In other words, the well-established relation between satisfaction and AC to the organization is mirrored between other constituencies in the military. Furthermore, these results support Hunt and Morgan's (1994) finding that organizational commitment is a mediating construct between commitment to collectives and organizationally relevant outcome variables. Specifically, in this research investigation, military AC mediated the relation between career intentions and both satisfaction with the military and Special Operations AC. Furthermore, there was a cross-constituency effect from satisfaction with Special Operations Forces to military AC.

Methodological Issues

Although a causal model was developed, tested with sophisticated statistical techniques, and supported by the analyses, the research design was nonexperimental. Caution should always be used in drawing causal inferences when time precedence cannot be established by experimental manipulation. Furthermore, a causal model often implies a developmental sequence. Although Mueller and Lawler (1999) hinted at the possibility of a developmental pattern, this is not the implication that should be drawn from our research. There are causal links in the model, but these links should not be interpreted as a model of the development of organizational commitment. Instead, the model displays a snapshot of how the salience of the proximal collective permits some attitudes (e.g., satisfaction, commitment) to be stronger and influences attitudes toward distal collectives. The developmental implications of the model remain to be tested within a longitudinal framework.

Additional concerns can be raised about the participants used in this research. The characteristics of the respondents are quite unique. Special Operations personnel are highly selected members of the military forces and do not fully represent the breadth of personnel in the military, much less in civilian organizations. Furthermore, the sample size used for this investigation is exceptionally large when compared to typical research designs. Because the significance tests used in this study are influenced by sample size, it is possible some findings may not be replicated in smaller scale investigations. Additional research using a broader range of military and civilian personnel should be conducted to further elaborate the theory of nested collectives.

Implications and Suggestions for Future Research

Despite the limitations of this investigation, several implications for military and civilian environments can be drawn. First, the abbreviated scales can be used as acceptable measures of the constructs. This research supports the distinction between the scales. This finding should be replicated with diverse populations.

Second, the commitment measures can be used for multiple constituencies with only minor modifications to represent the different collectives. The question still remains, "How many constituencies is too many?" Respondents in this research were able to make distinctions between two organizational collectives, but there may be a limit to the number of distinguishable collectives. What is the maximum number of assessable nested commitments before they become indistinguishable? Can the commitment measures be adapted to collectives that are not nested?

Finally, a satisfied and committed workforce tends to have low turnover. In an era of economic abundance, the military needs to foster retention to maintain a workforce to meet the required missions. This research suggests that enhancing satisfaction and commitment at a proximal level will also contribute to satisfaction and commitment to the military and thus to retention. Experts suggest that, in the future, soldiers will operate in smaller, more independent units similar to those currently found in Special Operations Forces. If positive teamwork in these units can be molded to increase satisfaction and commitment, then overall turnover may be reduced. This would lead to a more cohesive, satisfied, and committed group of military men and women prepared to meet any operational contingency.

ACKNOWLEDGMENTS

The authors would like to thank Eric Wetzel and Peter Ramsberger of the Human Resources Research Organization for their contributions to the design and administration of the questionnaire and sampling plan used in this research.

The views, opinions, and/or findings contained in this article are solely those of the authors and should not be construed as an official Department of the Army or DOD position, policy, or decision, unless so designated by other documentation.

REFERENCES

Anderson, J. C., & Gerbing, D. W. (1988). Structural equation modeling in practice: A review and recommended two-step approach. *Psychological Bulletin, 103,* 411–423.

Angle, H., & Perry, J. (1981). An empirical study of theories of organizational commitment and organizational effectiveness. *Administrative Science Quarterly, 26,* 1–14.

Barling, J., & Wade, B. (1990). Predicting employee commitment to the company and union: Divergent models. *Journal of Occupational Psychology, 63,* 49–61.

Becker, T. E. (1992). Foci and bases of commitment: Are they distinctions worth making? *Academy of Management Journal, 35,* 232–244.

Becker, T. E., Billings, R. S., Eveleth, D. M., & Gilbert, N. L. (1996). Foci and bases of employee commitment: Implications for job performance. *Academy of Management Journal, 39,* 464–482.

Bishop, J. W., & Scott, K. D. (2000). An examination of organizational and team commitment in a self-directed team environment. *Journal of Applied Psychology, 85,* 439–450.

Diana, M. (1998). *Work environment, career, and family influences on the reenlistment intentions of Army soldiers.* Unpublished doctoral dissertation, George Mason University, Fairfax, VA.

Ellermers, N., de Gilder, D., & van den Heuvel, H. (1998). Career-oriented versus team-oriented commitment and behavior at work. *Journal of Applied Psychology, 83,* 717–730.

Gade, P. A., Tiggle, R., & Schumm, W. R. (2003/this issue). The measurement and consequences of military organizational commitment in soldiers and spouses. *Military Psychology, 15,* 191–207.

COMMITMENT IN SPECIAL OPERATIONS FORCES

Gerbing, D. W., & Anderson, J. C. (1992). Monte Carlo evaluations of goodness of fit indices for structural equation models. *Sociological Methods and Research, 21,* 132–160.

Heffner, T. S., & Rentsch, J. R. (2001). Organizational commitment and social interaction: A multiple constituencies approach. *Journal of Vocational Behavior, 51,* 471–490.

Human Resources Research Organization. (1998). *PERSTEMPO Impact Survey.* Alexandria, VA: Author.

Hunt, S. D., & Morgan, R. M. (1994). Organizational commitment: One of many commitments or key mediating construct? *Academy of Management Journal, 37,* 1568–1587.

Johnston, I. D. (1988). *Turnover of junior Army officers: A test of the Mobley, Griffith, Hand, and Maglino model of personnel turnover using structural equation techniques.* Unpublished master's thesis, Naval Postgraduate School, Monterey, CA.

Lakhani, H., & Gade, P. A. (1992). Career decisions of dual military career couples: A multidisciplinary analysis of the U.S. Army. *Journal of Economic Psychology, 13,* 153–166.

Lawler, E. J. (1992). Affective attachment to nested groups: A choice process theory. *American Sociological Review, 57,* 327–339.

Lease, S. H. (1998). Annual review, 1993–1997: Work attitudes and outcomes. *Journal of Vocational Behavior, 53,* 154–183.

Mathieu, J. E., & Zajac, D. M. (1990). A review and meta-analysis of the antecedents, correlates, and consequences of organizational commitment. *Psychological Bulletin, 108,* 171–194.

McGee, G. W., & Ford, R. C. (1987). Two (or more?) dimensions of organizational commitment: Reexamination of the affective and continuance commitment scales. *Journal of Applied Psychology, 72,* 638–642.

Medsker, G. J., Williams, L. J., & Holahan, P. J. (1994). A review of current practices for evaluating causal models in organizational behavior and human resource management research. *Journal of Management, 20,* 439–464.

Meyer, J. P., & Allen, N. J. (1984). Testing the "side-bet theory" of organizational commitment: Some methodological considerations. *Journal of Applied Psychology, 69,* 372–378.

Meyer, J. P., & Allen, N. J. (1991). A three-component conceptualization of organizational commitment. *Human Resource Management Review, 1,* 61–89.

Meyer, J. P., & Allen, N. J. (1997). *Commitment in the workplace: Theory, research, and application.* Thousand Oaks, CA: Sage.

Motowidlo, S. J., & Lawton, G. W. (1984). Affective and cognitive factors in soldiers' reenlistment decisions. *Journal of Applied Psychology, 69,* 157–166.

Mueller, C. W., & Lawler, E. J. (1999). Commitment to nested organizational units: Some basic principles and preliminary findings. *Social Psychology Quarterly, 62,* 325–346.

Ostroff, C. (1993). Comparing correlations based on individual-level and aggregate data. *Journal of Applied Psychology, 78,* 569–582.

Pedhazur, E. J., & Schmelkin, L. P. (1991). *Measurement, design, and analysis: An integrated approach.* Hillsdale, NJ: Lawrence Erlbaum Associates, Inc.

Porter, L. W., Steers, R. M., Mowday, R. T., & Boulian, P. V. (1974). Organizational commitment, job satisfaction, and turnover among psychiatric technicians. *Journal of Applied Psychology, 59,* 603–609.

Reichers, A. E. (1985). A review and reconceptualization of organizational commitment. *Academy of Management Review, 10,* 465–476.

Reichers, A. E. (1986). Conflict and organizational commitments. *Journal of Applied Psychology, 71,* 508–514.

Rusbult, C. E., & Farrell, D. (1983). A longitudinal test of the investment model: The impact on job satisfaction, job commitment, and turnover on variations in rewards, costs, alternatives, and investments. *Journal of Applied Psychology, 68,* 429–438.

Schneider, B. (1985). Organizational behavior. *Annual Review of Psychology, 36,* 573–611.

Spector, P. E. (1997). *Job satisfaction: Application, assessment, causes, and consequences.* Thousand Oaks, CA: Sage.

Sterling, B., & Allen, J. (1983). *Relationships among organizational attitudes, work environment, satisfaction with human resource programs and benefits, and Army career intentions* (Tech. Rep. No. 572). Alexandria, VA: U.S. Army Research Institute for the Behavioral and Social Sciences. (DTIC No. AD–A139 864)

Vandenberg, R. J., & Scarpello, V. (1994). A longitudinal assessment of the determinant relationship between employee commitments to the occupation and the organization. *Journal of Organizational Behavior, 15,* 535–547.

MILITARY PSYCHOLOGY, 2003, *15*(3), 225–236
Copyright © 2003, Lawrence Erlbaum Associates, Inc.

Antecedents and Consequences of Organizational Commitment

Angela I. Karrasch
U.S. Army Research Institute

The purpose of this study was to examine some antecedents and some consequences of organizational commitment as conceptualized by Meyer and Allen (1991). Specifically, gender, ethnicity, branch of the Army, and perceptions of tokenism (e.g., isolation and stereotyping) were examined as antecedents of organizational commitment. Peer-rated leadership performance served as the outcome measure of affective (AC), continuance (CC), and normative commitment (NC). Findings indicated ethnic differences in AC and CC, gender differences in CC, and Army branch differences in AC and NC. Perceived tokenism was associated with lower levels of AC and NC and higher levels of CC. Finally, higher levels of AC and NC predicted higher leadership evaluations, whereas higher levels of CC were associated with lower leadership evaluations.

The Army often requires long hours, frequent relocation, multiple deployments, and the execution of life-threatening duties for an average amount of pay. That U.S. service men and women remain in the Army despite all these hardships may be largely explained by the concept of organizational commitment. Therefore, understanding the multifaceted nature of commitment and any factors that influence the development or outcomes of commitment to the Army is critical to maintaining a motivated and ready force.

Generally, there has not been enough research on antecedents of organizational commitment to make significant progress in understanding the development and process of commitment building. Research examining antecedents to commitment does exist, (e.g., Bateman & Strasser, 1984; Mathieu, 1991; Steers, 1977) and typically calls for more longitudinal designs. To my knowledge, tokenism as an antecedent to organizational commitment has not been examined.

Requests for reprints should be sent to Angela I. Karrasch, U.S. Army Research Institute, Armored Forces Research Unit, 2423 Morande Street, Ft. Knox, Kentucky, 40121-5620. E-mail: angela.karrasch@knox.army.mil.

Tokenism is promoted by disproportionate numbers in social categories and apparent "status" differences among the members of an organization (Yoder, 1994). It is characterized by the perception of isolation, stereotyping, and heightened visibility among members of the organization (Kanter, 1977). This is a phenomenon for which the military may be particularly vulnerable and one that could impact organizational commitment as well as performance.

The purpose of this study was to examine both perceptions of tokenism and some related demographics as predictors, as well as leadership performance as an outcome of the three components of organizational commitment as conceptualized by Meyer and Allen (1991).

Meyer and Allen (1997) suggested that, although all three components of commitment (affective, continuance, and normative) could increase the likelihood of soldiers remaining in the Army, there are different antecedents and consequences associated with each of these components.

PERCEIVED TOKENISM AS AN ANTECEDENT
OF ORGANIZATIONAL COMMITMENT

Previous research by Crocker and Major (1989) suggested that minority members of a group can actually selectively devalue attributes, abilities, events, and such that pose a threat to one's overall sense of worth. Selective devaluing has also been referred to as disidentification (Steele, 1997). If tokenism that makes an individual feel out of place or inept is prevalent in an organization, that individual may disidentify with the organization—or lower his or her commitment. This disidentification could subsequently have an impact on performance. The U.S. Army actually engineers some situations (e.g., classroom situations) such that women, ethnic minorities, and particular branches are "spread out," thus allowing more groups to be exposed to these individuals. Unfortunately, it sets up a tokenism situation for those minority individuals. As part of this study, perceptions of tokenism were examined to determine the impact on the various components of commitment. Although it seemed likely that high tokenism could lower one's feeling of belonging (affective commitment [AC]), it was difficult to predict how tokenism may impact one's feelings of loyalty (normative commitment [NC]) or perceptions of alternative comparisons (continuance commitment [CC]).

LEADERSHIP BEHAVIOR AS A CONSEQUENCE
OF ORGANIZATIONAL COMMITMENT

Much of the research on organizational commitment focuses on career intent. Career intent is an important correlate of organizational commitment; however, this relation has been firmly established by previous research. Allen and Meyer (1996) argued—and Gade, Tiggle, and Schumm (2003/this issue) showed—that part of the value of organizational commitment lies in the recognition that the components of commitment may have very different implications for various types of job-related behaviors. Allen and Meyer (1996) noted that employees with strong AC to their organization tend to "perform better, are absent from work less often, and engage more in good organizational citizenship behaviors" than those low in AC. In contrast, those with high CC have often performed work behaviors more poorly (e.g., Gade et al.).

This indicates that the military should be interested not only in commitment as it relates to retention but also in how commitment components relate to performance outcomes as well. The ability or willingness to lead is arguably one of the most important performance variables in military organizations. It was expected that high AC and NC would be positively related to high leader performance evaluations but that high CC would actually relate to lower leader performance evaluations.

METHOD

Participants

Surveys from 1,270 male and 142 female Army captains who attended a 6-week course at Combined Arms and Services Staff School (CAS³) at Fort Leavenworth, Kansas, were analyzed. This school provides training in advanced tactical decision making and division-level staff skills. The course involves a series of individual and group tasks, all designed to improve students' leadership abilities, communication skills, and decision-making ability; their understanding of Army organizations, operations, and procedures; and their ability to work as members of a staff.

Milieu of CAS³. Classes are divided into sections of 12 to 14 students. These sections are called *staff groups*. The members of each staff group spend long hours in and out of class together. They work, eat, dorm, do physical training, and socialize together. This environment seemed conducive for allowing peers to get to know, and be able to evaluate, their counterparts' leadership behaviors.

Demographics. Captains have served approximately 8 years in the service before they take this 6-week course. Overall, the women in this study were predominately White (71%), with the second major ethnic group being Black (25%). The majority of women belonged to the Combat Service Support branch (52%), which includes such specialties as law, ministry, medical service, transportation, supplies, and personnel management. Sixty-three women (44%) worked in Combat Support, which includes military intelligence, engineers, signal corps (communications), military police, chemical corps, and air defense artillery. Finally, there were 5 women (4%) in Combat Arms, which includes specialties such as aviation, special forces, armor, infantry, and field artillery (most of which are closed to female officers).

The men in this study were also predominately White (83%). One hundred eleven (9%) were Black. Most men (47%) represented the Combat Arms branch, 28% represented Combat Support, and 25% represented Combat Service Support. See Table 1 for more information on demographic variables by Army branch for men and women.

Procedures

CAS[3] instructors distributed surveys and provided a brief overview of this study. Class time was given to fill out the initial survey. When finished, students placed their surveys in envelopes, sealed them, and handed them to the instructor. The surveys were collected from the instructor.

The data on perceptions of tokenism, gender, ethnicity, and branch were collected during the first week of CAS[3]. Data on commitment and peer evaluations of leadership behaviors were collected 6 weeks later.

Measures

Task-specific peer evaluations. Participants were asked to rank their peers and themselves on each of four leadership items: (a) their respect for his or her ideas, opinions, and person; (b) their perception of his or her contribution to the

TABLE 1
Sample Frequencies by Branch of Service, Gender, and Ethnicity

| | Branch and Gender | | | | | | |
| | Combat Arms | | Combat Support | | Combat Service Support | | |
Ethnicity	Men	Women	Men	Women	Men	Women	Total
White	521	4	288	50	249	47	1159
Black	32	1	33	9	46	25	146
Hispanic	17	0	19	1	10	1	48
Asian	13	0	14	2	9	1	39
Native American	6	0	1	0	1	0	8
Other	4	0	4	1	3	0	12
Total	593	5	359	63	318	74	1,412

group effort; (c) their perception of his or her ability to lead the group; and (d) their perception of his or her technical–tactical competence. These four items assessing leadership provided the basis for deriving the peer evaluation of leadership scores.

A mean rank across the 11 to 13 peer rankings for each participant was calculated for each of the four leadership items described previously. This produced four mean peer evaluation ratings for each participant. The interrater reliability coefficients were as follows for each area of leadership: respect for his or her ideas, opinions, and person (.79); contribution to group effort (.79); ability to lead (.80); and technical–tactical competence (.81).

The second step of the procedure used to create a single peer evaluation score was to take the mean of the four leadership items. The interitem reliability among the four leadership items based on peer data was .93.

Perceived tokenism.   Perceived tokenism refers to the perceived aversive outcomes of skewed group proportions. Because perceived tokenism is not generally apparent to dominant members of a group, it is difficult to assess from their perspective. Therefore, perceived tokenism is generally measured by assessing the perceptions of the "tokens" themselves. Indeed, as the recipients of perceived negative outcomes of tokenism, they may be more aware of it than observers and dominants.

Thirteen statements describing tokenism were drawn from surveys used in previous studies of tokenism (Kanter, 1977; Ott, 1989; South, Bonjean, Markham, & Corder, 1982; Spangler, Gordon, & Pipkin, 1978; Yoder, Adams, & Prince, 1983, 1986; Yoder & Sinnett, 1985). Five statements were adapted to assess whether participants felt more visible or salient than other group members. A typical item representing this category was, "I received a disproportionate amount of attention or scrutiny from my peers." Four statements were adapted to assess the extent of isolation or polarization a participant felt. A typical item was, "I feel that I lack peer acceptance." Four statements were adapted to assess the extent to which a participant felt stereotypic treatment. A typical item was, "I felt that I was assigned tasks based on stereotyped assumptions about my branch, race, or gender."

Participants were asked to indicate on a scale from 1 (*never*) to 5 (*very often*) how often each of the 13 statements were descriptive of their career experiences thus far with the Army. A factor analysis indicated that two items ("My instructor or peers took special note of my competencies" and "I felt conspicuous") did not load well with the other items. To obtain a more internally consistent scale, these two items were deleted. The final scale consisted of 11 items and had a coefficient alpha of .76.

Commitment.   Three components of commitment were measured using slightly modified versions of the Allen and Meyer (1990) AC scale and the revised versions of the NC and CC scales (Meyer, Allen, & Smith, 1993). The modification involved inserting the name "Army" where "organization" was mentioned.

A three-factor model of organizational commitment was hypothesized and tested using LISREL (Jöreskog & Sörbom, 1993). The Affective factor specified consisted of the following six items: (a) "I would be very happy to spend the rest of my career in the Army"; (b) "I really feel as if the Army's problems are my own"; (c) "I do not feel like 'part of the family' in the Army"; (d) "I do not feel emotionally attached to the Army"; (e) "The Army has a great deal of personal meaning for me"; and (f) "I do not feel a strong sense of belonging in the Army."

The Continuance factor consisted of the following seven items: (a) "It would be very hard for me to leave the Army right now, even if I wanted to"; (b) "Too much of my life would be disrupted if I decided I wanted to leave the Army right now"; (c) "Right now, staying with the Army is a matter of necessity as much as desire"; (d) "I believe that I have too few options to consider leaving the Army"; (e) "One of the few negative consequences of leaving the Army would be the scarcity of available alternatives"; (f) "One of the major reasons I continue to be a soldier is that leaving the Army would require considerable personal sacrifice: Another organization may not match the overall benefits I have here."; and (g) "If I had not already put so much of myself into the Army I might consider working elsewhere."

The Normative factor consisted of the following six items: (a) "I do not feel any obligation to remain with the Army"; (b) "Even if it were to my advantage, I do not feel that it would be right to leave the Army now"; (c) "I would feel guilty if I left the Army right now"; (d) "The Army deserves my loyalty"; (e) "I would not leave the Army right now because I have a sense of obligation to the people in it"; and (f) "I owe a great deal to the Army."

All items were submitted to a confirmatory factor analysis (CFA) using LISREL. The CFA model is shown in Figure 1. The goodness of fit statistics indicated very marginal support for the three-factor model. The χ^2 of 1,905 was significant ($df = 149$), which could be expected with the large sample size ($N = 1,107$). The goodness of fit index (GFI) was .83 and the Root Mean Square Residual was .09. The modification indexes suggested a better fit would have been possible if error covariance between several of the items had been specified. The AC latent construct was strongly related to the NC construct ($r = .74$), but the correlation with CC construct ($r = .13$) was much more modest. NC and CC were moderately related ($r = .27$).

RESULTS

Gender

AC and NC did not vary significantly by gender. However, an analysis of variance (ANOVA) on CC indicated that men ($M = 2.54$) were significantly higher in CC than women ($M = 2.37$), $F(1, 1193) = 4.14$, $p < .05$, $r(1198) = .06$.

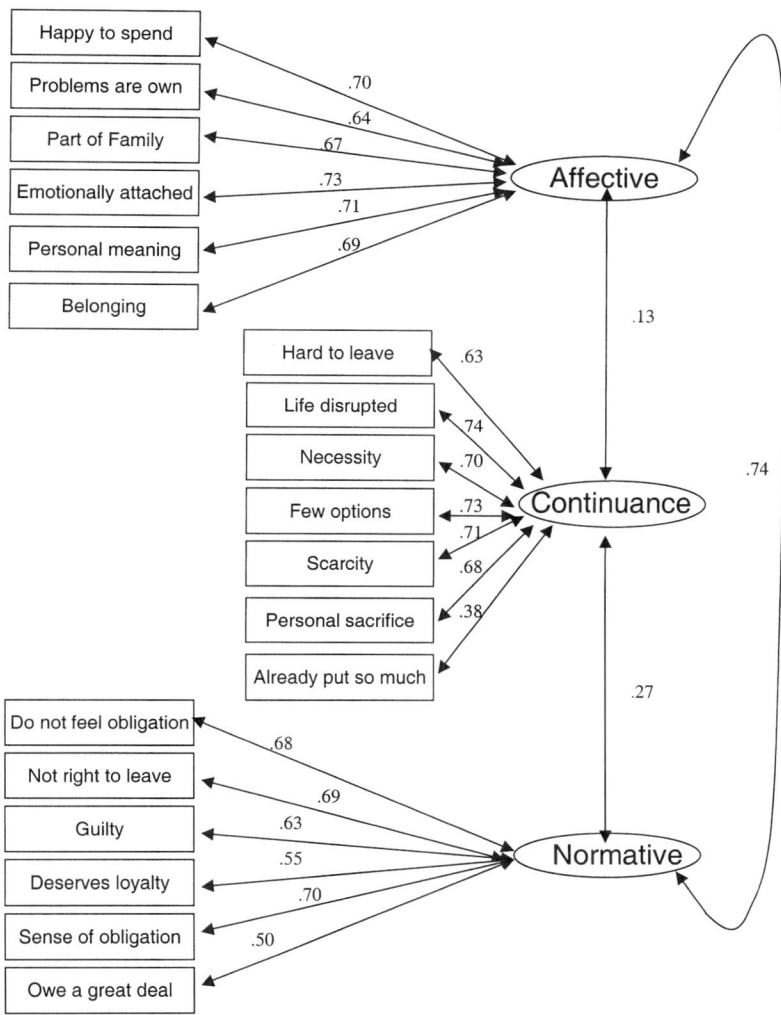

FIGURE 1. Results of a confirmatory factor analysis testing a three-factor model of organizational commitment.

Branch

AC levels, $F(2, 1195) = 4.64$, $p < .01$, $r(1198) = -.09$, and NC levels, $F(2, 1195) = 6.25$, $p < .002$, $r 1,198) = -.10$, were both significantly different by branch. For both AC and NC, the Combat Arms branch had the highest means ($M = 3.83$) and ($M = 3.35$), respectively, followed by Combat Support, and then Combat Service Support branches. CC did not differ significantly by branch of the Army.

Ethnicity

No significant differences were found in NC by ethnicity; however, AC, $F(5, 1192)$ = 2.38, $p < .04$, $r(1198) = -.02$ and CC, $F(5,1192) = 3.70$, $p < .01$, $r(1198) = .11$, both differed significantly by ethnicity.

Perceived Tokenism

Participants were divided into those reporting low or mild tokenism versus those reporting strong tokenism in their environment. There were significant differences in AC $F(1, 919) = 51.15$, $p < .05$, $r(1146) = -.28$ and CC levels $F(1,916) = 18.17$, $p < .05$, $r(1146) = .13$; however, there were no significant differences in NC by tokenism level. This analysis revealed that those reporting strong tokenism were significantly lower in AC ($M = 3.59$) than those reporting mild tokenism ($M = 3.94$). The opposite pattern appears with CC. Those reporting strong tokenism were higher in CC ($M = 2.62$) than those reporting mild tokenism ($M = 2.38$).

Table 2 presents the means, standard deviations, and correlations among all variables of interest in this study for a further examination of how these demographic and antecedent variables related to commitment and peer evaluations of leadership ability.

A path analyses model was tested to examine the influence of tokenism on the formation of each type of commitment and the influence of each type of commitment on leadership evaluations. The model was tested using LISREL and can be viewed in Figure 2.

The model indicates that tokenism is a modest predictor of all three forms of commitment and that commitment is a modest predictor of leadership ability. The

TABLE 2
Means, Standard Deviations, and Correlations Between Major Variables in This Study

Variable	M	SD	1	2	3	4	5	6	7	8
1. Affective	3.76	0.73	1.00							
2. Continuance	2.52	0.84	0.12**	1.00						
3. Normative	3.26	0.74	0.60**	0.24**	1.00					
4. Perceived Tokenism	2.21	0.52	−.28**	0.13**	−.08**	1.00				
5. Leadership	7.33	2.11	0.14**	−.07**	0.08**	−.17**	1.00			
6. Ethnicity			−.01	0.11**	0.03	0.14**	−.15**	1.00		
7. Branch			−.08**	0.02	−.10**	0.11*	−.33**	0.06*	1.00	
8. Gender			0.05	0.06**	0.04	−.08*	0.11**	−.02	−.26	1.00

Note. $*p < .05$, $**p = .01$

Scales are scored such that higher numbers indicate more affective, continuance and normative commitment, more perceived tokenism, more positive peer evaluations. Higher numbers are also associated with being non-white, non-combat arms, and male.

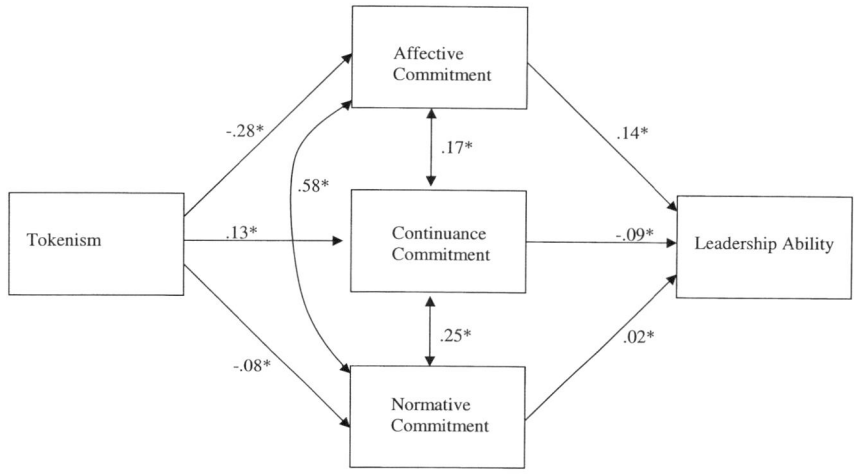

FIGURE 2. Results of the path analysis showing relation between tokenism, as an antecedent of each form of commitment, and leadership ability as an outcome of three forms of organizational commitment.

coefficients relating tokenism to AC and NC are negative. This indicates that more tokenism is related to less AC and NC, which in turn is related to lower leadership evaluations. Conversely, the model also indicates that lower leadership evaluations can be predicted by higher CC, which is predicted by more tokenism.

The LISREL goodness of fit statistics support this model. The χ^2 of 761.44 was significant ($df = 1$), which was not surprising, given the sample size ($N = 1,143$). The GFI was .97, the adjusted goodness of fit index (AGFI) was more conservative at .92, and the Root Mean Square Residual was .03. These statistics indicate that the data fit the model well.

DISCUSSION

Formation of Organizational Commitment

No specific hypotheses were examined regarding demographic variables in this particular study. However, an exploratory examination of those variables indicates it may be interesting to study why the differences existed within particular forms of commitment but not all forms of commitment. It is possible the particular antecedents examined in this study are confounds for more specific anteced- ents. For instance, finding that male soldiers are higher in CC than female sol- diers could be attributable to men having more years invested with the Army than women. Alternatively, male soldiers may be more likely to have spouses who do not work outside the home; therefore, the cost of leaving the Army and losing benefits may be higher for men as compared to female soldiers. Thus, finding ethnic differences in AC and CC, gender differences in CC, and branch differences in AC and NC may be just a starting point. In any case, demographic antecedents appear to have serious implications for the Army's ability to main- tain a motivated and ready force.

It was not surprising to find that those reporting stronger perceptions of token- ism also had lower AC to the Army. According to Steele (1997), the stereotype threat or isolation that tokens in this study might have experienced is a typical de- fense mechanism to buffer self-esteem and often leads to reduction in commitment or identification with a particular self-schema. It is interesting to note that higher tokenism was related to lower AC but also to higher CC. It is possible that those of- ficers experiencing tokenism do not feel like the Army is family but at the same time perceive that the civilian world does not offer a better alternative. This specu- lation is consistent with general perceptions within the Army that the military is more accepting of diversity than private industry and that the Army makes explicit efforts to promote based on merit alone.

Generally, findings from this study suggest that tokenism may actually inhibit the development of, or at least the expression of, AC and NCs that are positively re- lated to successful performance. On the other hand, perceived tokenism seems to facilitate CC that is related to lowered performance.

Performance Outcomes of Three Forms of Organizational Commitment

The results of the path analyses point to some commonalities and differences in the way that each form of commitment is influenced and manifested. For instance, AC appears to be a stronger predictor of leadership behavior than NC and is much more influenced by tokenism than NC. The model indicates that stronger percep- tions of tokenism are associated with declines in AC. A decline in AC is related to a decline in leadership behavior.

In contrast to AC and NC, CC is negatively associated with leadership behavior. Apparently, officers in this study who were evaluated as less willing or able to demonstrate leadership are still willing to remain in the army for lack of perceived alternatives. Obviously, this is not an ideal situation for the Army. Understanding the different forms of commitment and being able to identify methods for increas- ing AC may prove to be an integral task in improving leadership performance within the Army.

A final note concerning the measurement of organizational commitment: The data from the CFA indicated that a three-factor solution is not the best model for this data. In general, NC did not appear to provide much added value to this examination of officer commitment. In addition, in the majority of the analyses, NC demonstrated effects very similar to AC. However, the construct seems to have a lot of face validity, especially for an organization like the military. Furthermore, there appears to be some divergence regarding the development and consequences of AC and NC. Therefore, it is probably premature to rely solely on AC and continuance commitment when examining the formation and consequences of commitment to the Army.

REFERENCES

Allen, N. J., & Meyer, J. P. (1990). The measurement and antecedents of affective, continuance, and normative commitment to the organization. *Journal of Occupational Psychology, 63,* 1–18.

Allen, N. J., & Meyer, J. P. (1996). Affective, continuance, and normative commitment to the organization: An examination of construct validity. *Journal of Vocational Behavior, 49,* 252–276.

Bateman, T. S., & Strasser, S. (1984). A longitudinal analysis of the antecedents of organizational commitment. *Academy of Management Journal, 27,* 95–112.

Crocker, J., & Major, B. (1989). Social stigma and self-esteem: The self-protective properties of stigma. *Psychological Review, 96,* 608–630.

Gade, P. A., Tiggle, R., & Schumm, W. (2003/this issue). The measurement and consequences of military organizational commitment in soldiers and spouses. *Military Psychology, 15,* 191–207.

Jöreskog, K. G., & Sörbom, D. (1993). *LISREL 8: Structural equation modeling with the SIMPLIS command language.* Hillsdale, NJ: Lawrence Erlbaum Associates, Inc.

Kanter, R. M. (1977). Some effects of proportions on group life: Skewed sex ratios and responses to token women. *American Journal of Sociology, 82,* 965–990.

Karrasch, A. I. (1999). *The effects of tokenism on task-specific self-evaluations and global self-esteem.* Unpublished doctoral dissertation, Kansas State University, Manhattan, KS.

Mathieu, J. (1991). A cross-level non-recursive model of the antecedents of organizational commitment and satisfaction. *Journal of Applied Psychology, 76,* 607–618.

Meyer, J. P., & Allen, N. J. (1991). A three component conceptualization of organizational commitment. *Human Resource Management Review, 1,* 61–98.

Meyer, J. P., & Allen, N. J., (1997). *Commitment in the workplace: Theory, research and application.* Thousand Oaks, CA: Sage.

Meyer, J. P., Allen, N. J., & Smith, C. A. (1993). Commitment to organizations and occupations: Extension and test of a three component conceptualization. *Journal of Applied Psychology, 78,* 538–551.

Ott, E. M. (1989). Effects of male-female ratio at work. *Psychology of Women Quarterly, 13,* 41–57.

Spangler, E., Gordon, M. A., & Pipkin, R. M. (1978). Token women: An empirical test of Kanter's hypothesis. *American Journal of Sociology, 84,* 160–169.

South, S. J., Bonjean, C. M., Markham, W. T., & Corder, J. (1982). Social structure and intergroup interaction: Men and women of the federal bureaucracy. *American Sociological Review, 47,* 587–599.

Steele, C. M. (1997). A threat in the air: How stereotypes shape intellectual identity and performance. *American Psychologist, 52,* 613–629.

Steers, R. M. (1977). Antecedents and outcomes of organizational commitment. *Administrative Science Quarterly, 22,* 46–56.

Yoder, J. D. (1994). Looking beyond the numbers: The effects of gender status, job prestige, and occupational gender typing on tokenism processes. *Social Psychology Quarterly, 57,* 150–159.

Yoder, J. D., Adams, J., & Prince, H. T. (1983). The price of a token. *Journal of Political and Military Sociology, 11,* 325–337.

Yoder, J. D., & Sinnett, L. M. (1985). Is it all in the numbers? A case study of tokenism. *Psychology of Women Quarterly, 9,* 413–418.

ACKNOWLEDGMENTS

This article was based on a doctoral dissertation completed at Kansas State University.

I would like to thank retired Colonel Albert E. Bryant, former director of curriculum at the Combined Arms and Services Staff School who made it possible to collect these data. I would also like to thank Stan Halpin, Paul Gade, Catherine Cozzarelli and Bob Solick for their valuable input.

The views, opinions, and/or findings contained in this article are solely those of the author and should not be construed as an official Department of the Army or DOD position, policy, or decision, unless so designated by other documentation.

MILITARY PSYCHOLOGY, 2003, *15*(3), 237–253

Organizational Commitment in the Military: A Discussion of Theory and Practice

Natalie J. Allen
Department of Psychology
The University of Western Ontario

It is both a pleasure and a challenge to discuss the body of work that appears in this issue of *Military Psychology*. Taken together, it encompasses a wide scope, both substantively and methodologically. Various commitment-related issues are addressed, including the conceptualization and assessment of work commitment among military personnel, its behavioral consequences for those personnel (and hence those they serve), and the impact on commitment of military policies and practices. Further, the research makes scientific and practical contributions, reminding us that the blending of the two is both possible and desirable within applied research. Finally, for military "outsiders" like me, the issue represents an opportunity to add to one's repertoire of acronyms, always a humbling experience.

The following discussion is organized around four general themes. Three of these will be familiar to those who follow the commitment literature; the fourth is more specific to the military context. Within each theme, I offer a mix of observations about the relevant research, noting strengths, challenging assumptions, and raising specific questions. In addition, and rather more presumptuously, I identify directions that work commitment research in the military may usefully take in the future. Before beginning, I feel compelled to note my bias toward a three-component model of commitment that John Meyer and I developed several years ago. According to the model, the commitment an individual feels toward an entity, such as an organization, can be thought of in terms of three psychological ties that bind: emotional attachment (affective commitment [AC]), perceived costs associated with leaving (continuance commitment [CC]), and feelings of obligation (norma-

Requests for reprints should be sent to Natalie J. Allen, Department of Psychology, The University of Western Ontario; London, Ontario, Canada N6A 5C2. E-mail: nallen@uwo.ca.

tive commitment [NC]). Further, it is argued that the three components of the commitment profile develop on the basis of different antecedents and, beyond their link with staying or leaving, have different consequences for behavior.

CONCEPTUAL AND MEASUREMENT ISSUES WITHIN MILITARY COMMITMENT RESEARCH: BUILDING ON THEORY

As noted by Gade, Tiggle, and Schumm (2003/this issue), military commitment research has not tended to use measures developed within a theoretical context. Thus, less than ideal attention has been given to construct development and validation, a problem that challenges much organizational research (e.g., Hinkin, 1995, 1998; Schwab, 1980). Fortunately, a concern with conceptual and measurement issues is a predominant theme that emerges in this body of research.

If we take seriously the arguments about the organizational and individual consequences of workplace commitment, these efforts are very well placed. Early commitment research was characterized by various definitions and little attention to explication of the commitment construct (regardless of its definition). In addition to creating a very confusing literature, it has been argued that some of the mixed findings about the behavioral consequences of commitment can be traced to conceptual and measurement inconsistencies associated with the construct (Allen & Meyer, 2000; Meyer & Allen, 1997; Morrow, 1993). Although there is some controversy about the specific details, there is now near consensus in the literature that commitment to the organization is best viewed as having more than one dimension or component (Mayer & Schoorman, 1992; Meyer & Allen, 1991; O'Reilly & Chatman, 1986). Until recently, however, the dimensionality issue has received scant examination within military research. Thus, it has not been possible to examine the interrelations of these hypothesized dimensions or to assess their correlates within this setting. One might expect the general pattern of relations seen in the literature to generalize to the military context, but this is by no means assured. Moreover, given the size and breadth of its samples, military research has enormous potential to address other substantive gaps in our knowledge of work commitment. For all these reasons, military commitment research that takes a more systematic and theory-driven approach to measurement represents a most welcome contribution to the scientific literature.

In addition to concerns about scientific issues, practical issues also challenge applied researchers, of course. Consequently, efforts to evaluate various measures and techniques for assessing commitment and related variables, in settings such as the military, are very important. The ideal situation, most researchers would agree, is one in which such evaluations are done systematically and in light of existing theory. Happily, this is the case in this body of research.

The Organizational Commitment Construct: Dimensionality and Measurement

Although not their primary focus, several studies provide data relevant to the dimensionality issue. Of these, however, only Karrasch (2003/this issue) assessed all three components of commitment. In her study of Army captains, she used a slightly modified version of the original AC scale (Allen & Meyer, 1990; Meyer & Allen, 1984) and the shorter (revised) measures of the other two constructs (Meyer, Allen, & Smith, 1993). Results of a confirmatory factor analysis (CFA) of the commitment items provided some—although by no means unequivocal—support for the expected three-factor structure. Indeed, although the fit with a two-factor structure (with AC and NC on one factor and CC on the other) was not reported, the apparent relation between AC and NC items suggests that this may well have provided a superior fit to the data. Thus, although it appears that AC, CC, and NC are discernible by military personnel, the overall pattern is less clear than would be expected based on existing theory. This raises an interesting question about what NC to a military organization might mean; at this point, however, I agree with Karrasch that the decision to conceptualize commitment to the Army in terms of only AC and CC would be premature.[1]

Construct dimensionality was examined in conjunction with the development and use of alternate measures of AC and CC in three studies. The Gade et al. research involved an impressively broad set of data collected from both active and reservist members of Multinational Force and Observers (MFO) samples and from active Army officers and soldiers as part of the regularly administered Sample Survey of Military Personnel (SSMP). Measures of AC and CC, adapted slightly from those used previously (Allen & Meyer, 1990; Meyer & Allen, 1984), were administered to MFO personnel both predeployment and after they returned from peacekeeping duties in the Sinai. Experimental, abbreviated versions of these were also administered to members of the Special Operations Forces who participated in the study conducted by Heffner and Gade (2003/this issue). Finally, Tremble, Payne, Finch, and Bullis (2003/this issue) examined the dimensionality issue using adapted versions of the original AC and CC scales and the analog commitment measures developed in their study.

Results of the CFA that Gade et al. conducted on the "modified original" AC and CC items generally support the notion that Army personnel can distinguish between these two components of organizational commitment. A primary goal of this analysis, however, was to inform the selection of items for abbreviated (four-item) measures of AC and CC. The performance of these abbreviated measures, used in three

---

[1]It is worth noting that the revised version of the Normative Commitment Scale (NCS; Meyer et al., 1993), used by Karrasch, has typically been more strongly correlated with AC than has the original NCS (see Meyer, Stanley, Herscovitch, & Topolnytsky, 2002).

samples (Gade et al.; Heffner & Gade) is especially noteworthy. First, despite having fewer items, the reliability of both measures stacks up well against their longer counterparts. Second, CFA results reported by Gade et al. from SSMPs on post-Sinai MFOs, as well as Heffner and Gade's work with Special Operations Forces, confirm that the data well fit a two-factor (AC and CC) model.

Taken together, this research suggests that military personnel can distinguish among AC, CC, and NC to the military and that the abbreviated measures of the former two constructs have considerable promise. In applied settings when survey space is often at a premium, short scales are always welcome. Of course, a comprehensive evaluation of whether the gain in efficiency has any other psychometric consequences lies in the future. Two issues are worthy of particular attention in this regard. The first is that when assessed using the shorter scales, AC and CC are more highly correlated than is typically found with the original measures (see Allen & Meyer, 1996; Meyer et al., 2002). Although it is not clear whether this has a substantive explanation (e.g., something inherent to the military) or is due to slight item adaptations (e.g., the use of positively keyed items only or minor wording changes), it is something worth tracking in subsequent samples.

The second issue involves the dimensionality of the CC measure. Over the years, much debate and empirical attention has focused on what Meyer and Allen referred to in 1997 as an "unresolved issue" (e.g., Hackett, Bycio, & Hausdorf, 1994; McGee & Ford, 1987; Meyer, Allen, & Gellatly, 1990; Somers, 1993). Do the "low alternative" and "high sacrifice" items in the Continuance Commitment Scale (CCS) together create a unidimensional measure of CC? Or do they represent two distinguishable components of commitment? The accumulating data, as well as closer conceptual attention to the CC construct, suggests that both perspectives may be suboptimal. Indeed, it has been noted recently (Allen & Meyer, 2000) that the low alternative percept does not represent the psychological tie known as CC, per se, but rather one of its possible antecedents. Thus, strong CC may develop on the basis of perceptions of low alternatives but is not defined in terms of these perceptions. Empirically, this is borne out in a recent meta-analysis showing that turnover intention—a key consequence of commitment—is negatively related to the High Sacrifices subscale but not related to the Low Alternatives subscale (Meyer et al., 2002). With this in mind, Allen and Meyer (2000) recently suggested that future refinements to the CCS measure exclude explicit low alternative items. At a minimum, in subsequent research it may be useful to look closely at the abbreviated CCS and, in particular, to explore the implications of treating perceived alternatives as a potential antecedent, rather than a facet, of the CC construct.

The intriguing work of Tremble et al. also examines conceptual and measurement issues from a theory-driven perspective. Moreover, it aptly illustrates that there is more than one way to approach a problem. The primary goal of this project was ambitious—to determine whether previously collected data, using items that were not developed with AC or CC in mind, could serve as the basis for the development of analog measures of these constructs. If successful, this would allow for the examination of a large archival data set collected over several years and to do so in a way that builds on existing commitment theory. From this archive, subject-matter experts selected items with content judged to match that of the AC and CC scales. These "analog measures" were then evaluated with respect to their psychometric properties and hypotheses the authors derived from the commitment literature as well as by comparison with the behavior of the original measures. Like the abbreviated measures described earlier, the analog measures developed here show considerable promise in that they performed in accordance with theory. These new scales are reliable (both within and across time periods) and are related to other variables in a manner generally consistent with expectations. Further, factor analytic results showed that AC and CC could be distinguished from each other. Interestingly, however, the results of CFAs that Tremble et al. conducted on the three waves of data from the target sample support the superiority of a three-factor model over a two-factor model and, thus, add to the debate surrounding the dimensionality of the CC construct.[2] Consistent with the analog approach, Tremble et al. used the original measures as the benchmarks against which they judged the analog measures. These analyses suggested that the analog AC underrepresented the AC construct and the analog CC measure included variance that was extraneous to the CC construct. Given the generally impressive overall performance of the new measures, one could argue that Tremble et al. have taken a fairly conservative (albeit admirable) position. However, their concerns quite properly focus attention on the substantive content of the items in the analog scales. Of course, it is always easier to speculate after the fact —as I have the luxury of doing here. Examination of the analog AC measure suggests that what may be missing are items that reflect the emotion that strongly affective employees feel toward their organization. Such employees care deeply about maintaining their membership in the organization, not just for its extrinsic rewards but because they really like the organization.

Understanding potential problems with the analog CC scale is somewhat more complex. At first blush, it may appear that the measure captures too much of the low alternatives notion and not enough, perhaps, of the sacrifice notion. (Four of the seven items are denoted as "low alternatives" and a fifth item—"It would be difficult for me to find a good civilian job right now, considering my own qualifications and current labor market conditions"—also seems to reflect this.) This likely plays some role, although closer scrutiny of these items suggests that some also include "sacrifice" content. Possibly, the more serious concern about the analog CC

---

[2] Based on the meta-analysis mentioned previously, one would expect high sacrifice items to be related more strongly to turnover intention than low alternative items. Interestingly, although Tremble et al. observed this with the original continuance items, the analog measures produced the opposite pattern. In both the test and target samples, turnover intention correlated more strongly with the alternative than the sacrifice items (S. Payne, personal communication, September 7, 2001).

scale items involves their specificity. CC is the degree to which the employee rec-
ognizes, or is aware, that she or he is staying because of the costs associated with
leaving—not the existence of the costs themselves. Further, and critically, this
awareness can stem from various events or perceptions, the nature or substance of
which can be quite idiosyncratic to the individual. For this reason, the best CC
items are those that capture the recognition of perceived costs but do so without
reference to their specific source. Put another way, because this idiosyncrasy exists, it is easy to come up with continuance items that are overly specific and, thus,
miss the mark. Consider, for example, the analog item: "Personal freedom is better
in the military, compared to a civilian job that I could realistically expect to get."
Presumably, it focuses on the idea that leaving the military may require a sacrifice
in personal freedom. This item will successfully capture CC for a person who be-
lieves that this is the case and who places a lot of value on personal freedom (and
thus is psychologically bound by its potential sacrifice). What of someone who ac-
knowledges the potential loss but who places much less value on this organizational attribute? This person, too, will likely strongly endorse the item—even
though freedom, per se, contributes little to his or her psychological bond with the
organization. In other words, she or he will be accurately responding to the item in
question but, in doing so, may be overreporting true CC. A third person may well
believe that personal freedom is not any better in other jobs but, for other idiosyncratic reasons, feels bound to stay with the military. How does this person with
true, strong CC respond to such an item? Possibly by disagreeing with it and, in doing so, potentially underreporting CC.

Clearly, there are special challenges associated with the CC construct as both
this, and earlier, research illustrates. Having said that, it is important to stress, as
Tremble et al. have done, that the analog approach can be successful only to the extent that the appropriate items exist in the data set from which they are drawn. The
item pool these researchers used was not developed with the AC and CC constructs
in mind. Despite these challenges, their data provide additional evidence that the
AC–CC distinction is a meaningful one in the military and that there is more than
one way to assess these constructs.

Other Related Issues

Before leaving this theme, I would like to comment on two additional conceptual–measurement issues. First, Gade et al. collected commitment data from the
spouses of military personnel. To my knowledge, this strategy has not been used previously in the literature, and although the authors wisely point out that the small sample makes it inappropriate to draw strong conclusions about the data, this aspect of
the study invites speculation and raises several intriguing questions. Perhaps most
basic is one that touches on the constructs themselves. What does it mean to describe
another person's commitment? Can a person provide valid reports of the commitment felt by another? Whose commitment is really being assessed? With respect to

the latter, scrutiny of the CC measure suggests that it may comprise two constructs: the spouse's perception of his or her partner's CC to the military and the spouse's own CC to his or her partner's membership in the military. Despite this concern, note that for both AC and CC, the "matched" spouse–soldier measures are positively correlated, thus providing some evidence of convergent validity for both spouse measures. In addition, evidence of their discriminant validity comes from the findings that both crossover correlations (soldier AC–spouse CC, soldier CC–spouse AC) are nonsignificant, as would be expected. Also interesting is that less overlap exists between AC and CC in the soldier sample than in the spouse sample. Perhaps this simply indicates that you know yourself best and thus can see and make finer grained psychological distinctions better than someone else can—even one who, presumably, knows you very well. Using a larger sample, it would be interesting to see whether the length of time that couples have been together influences the overlap between spouse reports of the two constructs. Finally, in future work, a discussion about the practical uses of spousal commitment measures would be interesting. Presumably, commitment expressed by the persons themselves will always be a better predictor of most outcomes of interest. Can spouse commitment serve as a surrogate if this is not available? Or possibly to increment prediction? Would it be worthwhile to examine the commitment spouses themselves feel to the idea of their partner staying in the military? Second, Gade et al. collected commitment data using telephone interviews. This offers a practical solution to time and response rate problems that are often associated with traditionally administered questionnaires. It would be interesting, however, to see how commitment data collected in this manner compare to those collected via written questionnaires. Do the lack of anonymity and the personal contact in any way alter how employees respond?

CORRELATES OF COMMITMENT: EXPLORING CONSEQUENCES AND ANTECEDENTS

The second theme represented in this research reflects an interest in those correlates of commitment that are hypothesized to be its consequences and antecedents. The traditional caveat here is that, as in much work of this nature, although the variables examined in research are described as antecedents and consequences of commitment (and, logically, seem to deserve such), the research designs do not allow for causal conclusions implied by such language.

Consequences: Career Intent and Beyond

Although a growing body of research evidence has muted somewhat the debate about whether commitment matters, there is still much to be learned about its consequences for both work-related and non-work-related outcomes. One such consequence, career intent (or turnover intention), has been examined in relation to commitment in all the articles in this issue. Given that personnel retention is a critically important human resource issue within the military, this emphasis is not at all surprising. Despite considerable variation in how commitment is conceptualized and assessed across this research, a similar pattern—entirely consistent with commitment theory—is observed. Strongly committed employees are significantly less likely than those with weaker commitment to express an intent to leave the military.

When placed within the wider context of the commitment literature, this focus on turnover intention prompts two comments. First, turnover intention is the most clearly established correlate (or consequence) of organizational commitment. Thus, although it is useful to know that the relation holds up in military samples, such information perhaps adds less to the scientific literature than might other pieces of information. This is not to suggest, of course, that turnover intention need not be assessed in military research. Such measures are relatively quick and easy to collect and can serve multiple research and human resources purposes. In this research, for example, demonstrating an empirical link with turnover intention represented a critical piece in the construct validation process for newly developed or modified measures of organizational commitment (e.g., Gade et al.; Heffner & Gade; Tremble et al.) and commitment to other units (Heffner & Gade). Second, it is important that we keep in mind that intentions and behaviors are not the same thing (if only they were!). Thus, in addition to intentions, it would be useful for military researchers, wherever possible, to track and examine actual staying or leaving behavior. Particularly valuable would be analyses of commitment in light of the reasons for, and the timing of, departures (i.e., survival analysis; Morita, Lee, & Mowday, 1993). Such research would exemplify well how the resources that the military could bring to a problem—large numbers, longitudinal data collection, a sophisticated personnel tracking system—could be used to great advantage, informing applied researchers and theory builders alike.

As important as retention is, however, it is critical to think beyond the stay–leave issue. Indeed, how well an employee performs is just as important as, if not more important than, whether she or he plans to stay with the organization. If there is value in the three-component model, it resides, at least in part, in the emphasis it gives to other on-the-job behaviors and in the recognition that the three components of commitment may have different implications for these behaviors. Further, because every employee has some degree of AC, CC, and NC to the organization, it makes sense to consider how the components jointly influence these behaviors.

Both Karrasch and Gade et al. looked beyond career intent for possible outcomes of organizational commitment. Karrasch examined AC, CC, and NC of Army captains attending a lengthy training course. Citing the importance of leadership in the military, she focused on this aspect of performance. A particularly impressive aspect of this study is the leader behavior measure. Ratings were not done by subordinates, but by peers. Although one could argue that subordinates' ratings of leaders are more critical, it must be emphasized that the peers in this study —leaders themselves—are subject-matter experts and, thus, very credible evaluators. Further, for each participant, Karrasch collected ratings on four aspects of leader behavior from each of 11 to 13 peers, and evaluations were made after peers had been together on course for 6 weeks. Thus, performance measures reflect multiple ratings and multiple aspects of leadership, made by raters with considerable experience with the ratee and considerable experience with the leadership construct. Consistent with theory, Karrasch reported that AC and, to a lesser extent, NC were *positively* related to leader behavior and CC was *negatively* related to it.

This study is one of the first to examine relations between perceptions of leader behavior and the three components of organizational commitment and, thus, is an important addition to this literature. Because Karrasch's particular interest was in evaluating whether relations between perceptions of token status (within a group) and leader performance are mediated by each of the three components of commitment, it was necessary to examine the components separately. Given the sample size, however, it would be possible, and quite interesting, to examine leader behavior as a function of the AC–CC–NC profile mentioned earlier.

Those interested in the consequences of organizational commitment will find at least two aspects of the Gade et al. work particularly notable. First, they examined a variety of outcome measures. In addition to the career intent measure mentioned previously, their study included two measures of job knowledge (assessed using objective tests), self-reported readiness to perform wartime duties, and self-reported morale. (From a construct perspective, the latter seems somewhat problematic. Although described as an index of well-being, it may be that some well-being researchers would take some exception to this—e.g., Sevastos, Smith, & Cordery, 1992. Moreover, some conceptual overlap between commitment and morale seems likely.) Second, relations between commitment and these measures were examined by considering AC and CC jointly—something that is rare in the literature (e.g., Meyer, Paunonen, Gellatly, Goffin, & Jackson, 1989). Although based on a fairly small MFO sample (the four profile groups ranged from $N = 40$ to $N = 65$), the finding that AC and CC exert differential, additive effects on job knowledge is interesting. On both knowledge tests, the highest scores were obtained by individuals with a High Affective, Low Continuance profile (HALC) and the lowest for those with a Low Affective, High Continuance (LAHC) profile. The much larger SSMP data set was used to examine readiness and morale or well-being. For both measures, AC and CC interacted such that those with a HALC profile had the highest scores on both measures.

Beyond the general notion that AC and CC may differentially predict performance-related outcomes, neither prior theorizing, nor, obviously, an extensive database provides much specific guidance about what might have been expected here. Thus, Gade et al. are breaking new ground with these analyses. In anticipation that others will build on this work by conducting similar analyses, additional detail about exactly how the profile groups were created would be useful. Specifically, within each survey (MFO or SSMP), it is not clear whether the median splits used to assign personnel to each of the four profiles were based on the entire distribution of commitment data from the survey in question or only from those personnel for whom both commitment and outcome measures were collected. In a related vein, it would be interesting to know how much the distributions of AC and CC (and hence their median scores) differed across the two samples. Would it have made sense, for example, to pool the two samples and establish median splits on that basis?

In future research, examinations of the consequences of various commitment profiles will likely be cast in both substantive and methodological terms. For example, when an organization (or the field) settles on how best to assess commitment, and sufficient data are collected, subgrouping based on norms, rather than sample-specific data, may make sense. In addition, some interesting methodological challenges will be presented when commitment profiles also include commitment to foci other than the organization (e.g., department, team, occupation). Clearly, there is much to learn about the consequences of particular commitment profiles. In this regard, military researchers are well placed to provide considerable research leadership.

Impacts on Commitment

Antecedents, development, causes, predictors. All of these appear regularly in the titles of research articles that deal with workplace commitment. In addition to reflecting our strong interest in understanding, developing, and managing committed employees, the preponderance of this research reflects the diversity of variables that has been considered to have an impact on commitment. This includes characteristics of the person, the job or work, the organization (see Mathieu & Zajac, 1990; Meyer & Allen, 1997; Meyer et al., 2002, Mowday, Steers & Porter, 1979 for reviews), and, though to a lesser degree, process variables, such as person–organization fit (e.g., Finegan, 2000; Meyer, Irving, & Allen, 1998), and attributional factors (e.g., Koys, 1991). In this issue, two articles contribute to our understanding of what impacts on commitment. Because the Heffner and Gade work is discussed in some detail in the following section, the focus here is on the study done by Karrasch. This study is particularly interesting in that it deals with variables that are very topical and have implications for policy considerations.

Karrasch's particular interest lay in understanding whether organizational commitment can be influenced by social—and organizational—demographic factors. In addition to increasing our understanding of commitment, information of this nature can have both practical and political interest as organizations grapple with the challenges associated with workforce diversity. Specifically, Karrasch examined relations among the three components of commitment and several diversity-relevant variables: gender, ethnicity, branch of the military (Combat Arms, Combat Support, Combat Service Support), and the degree to which the individual perceives that he or she is a token. She hypothesized that minority status members (women, non-White, those not in Combat Arms) and those with strong perceived tokenism scores would have weaker AC and NC and stronger CC. Although the pattern was not completely consistent with this, and effects were modest, some support for these predictions was reported.

This research provides much food for thought about a complex issue. Like many antecedents studies, it prompts speculation about process. How are the variables examined here expected to influence each of the components of organizational commitment? Through what psychological processes might this occur? The theoretical basis for suggesting a link among these variables and AC seems somewhat straightforward. Within the Army (and, particularly, among Army captains), women and minority group members (non-White) represent a numerical minority, as do those who are not in Combat Arms. Moreover, minority status (and perceived tokenism) has been associated, in some research, with psychological discomfort and a feeling that one is not getting much support. Thus, if we make the assumption that such is the case in the military, the suggestion that such variables will be negatively related to AC makes theoretical sense. Moreover, some of the items in the perceived tokenism measure hint at this, for example, "I feel that I lack peer acceptance." (To make the same argument with respect to the minority status variables, of course, one would need to see evidence that a lack of support, acceptance, or the like mediates their links with AC.) When one considers the other components of commitment, however, the picture is less clear. Indeed, there seems little theoretical basis for expecting these variables to be related positively to CC and negatively to NC. How does a greater sense of tokenism within an organization increase one's feeling that leaving the organization would be costly? Why would people who do not consider themselves tokens have stronger feelings of obligation to remain with the organization than those who do?

To help understand this complexity, greater explication of the perceived tokenism construct, and its assessment, would be especially welcome. *Perceived tokenism* is defined here as "the perceived aversive outcomes of skewed group proportions" (Karrasch, 2003/this issue, p. 229). This definition appears, potentially, to incorporate both parts of a cause-and-effect sequence, reflecting both the extent to which one (a) is in a skewed group situation and (b) perceives it to have negative outcomes. Nonetheless, Karrasch provides a clear description of the items used in a the measure and makes reference to a factor analysis (presumably exploratory) that justifies the inclusion of all but two items in the measure. We are also told that, because perceived tokenism is difficult to assess from the perspective of those who are numerically dominant group members (i.e., non-tokens), the construct "is generally measured by assessing the perceptions of the 'tokens' themselves" (Karrasch, 2003/this issue, p. 229). Given this, it was somewhat puzzling that the relevant analyses included all participants in the study, tokens and non-tokens alike. From a construct validation perspective, and relevant to this latter point, it might be useful to draw particular attention to the relations between "actual" minority status (gender, ethnicity, branch) and the perceived token measure; as Karrasch shows in Table 2 (2003/this issue), each of these relations was significant and in the expected direction.

As is illustrated by the research discussed in this section, there are many ways to address questions about the consequences of commitment to the organization and the ways in which it is shaped and altered. Further, this research reminds us that commitment is related to both retention and other important behaviors. Finally, it makes salient that the military, like other organizations, is undergoing changes in the size and demographic composition of its workforce and that these changes can greatly challenge the ability to develop and retain committed personnel.

THE FOCI OF COMMITMENT

The final substantive theme reflects a concern with the "commitment to what?" question. Early commitment research focused on the organization and, within a somewhat different tradition, the occupation or profession. More recent theorizing, however, has emphasized that one can be committed to many work-related domains, or foci, and that workplace commitment is best understood by considering these in concert (e.g., Meyer & Allen, 1997; Meyer, Allen, & Topolnytsky, 1998; Mueller, Wallace, & Price, 1992). These include constituencies that are within (e.g., unit, team, department) and beyond (occupation, union, one's personal career) the organization as well as, of course, the organization itself. If we view psychological commitment as a multidimensional construct, as many researchers do, the extension of the construct to multiple foci greatly increases its complexity.

Given this complexity, it is not surprising that the body of empirical multiple foci research is still fairly small and that it represents various conceptualizations of commitment, rendering cross-study comparisons somewhat difficult (e.g., Becker & Billings, 1993; Hunt & Morgan, 1994; Irving, Coleman, & Cooper, 1997; Meyer et al., 1993; Mueller & Lawler, 1999). Indeed, only occupational commitment and organizational commitment, both viewed in affective terms, have received enough joint attention to warrant meta-analytic examination (Lee, Carswell, & Allen, 2000). Arguably, examining these two particular commitment foci is less challenging than the task taken on by Heffner and Gade in their work on commitment to nested foci (or collectives). In this research, which represents the only explicit look at the foci issue described herein, Heffner and Gade examined work attitudes among personnel in the military who were also members of Special Operations Forces. AC and CC to the military were assessed using the abbreviated measures discussed earlier; the former was modified simply by changing "military" to "Special Operations," thus creating a measure of AC with a different focus.

A pertinent question here is whether the military, and the Special Operations Forces nested within it, represent psychologically distinct foci to these personnel. Results of CFA suggest that they do—personnel were indeed able to distinguish, affectively, between these two foci. (And, as mentioned in the earlier dimensionality discussion, CC to the military was also differentiated in this analysis.) This finding raises three issues. The first, a small methodological one, relates to any study in which commitment to more than one focus is assessed on the same questionnaire and using parallel measures. Specifically, when foci differentiation is made quite salient (via the use of close-to-identical items), respondents may feel a demand to provide differential responses. To examine this, one could collect matched data in two separate data collection efforts. Likely, the CFA finding would replicate; nonetheless, it would be useful to rule out the possibility that this is an artifact of the research design.

Second, and at a more substantive level, the fact that personnel distinguish between the two commitment foci means that individuals could have strong AC to their Special Operations Force but not to the military as a whole (or vice versa). What implications might this have for retention? It seems unlikely that an individual would express low AC to the organization by leaving it because doing so would also mean leaving the unit nested within it. It is possible, however, that the reverse situation could prompt personnel to request reassignments or transfers within the organization. In extreme (albeit rare) cases, where a substantial difference exists between the levels of AC felt toward the larger and smaller foci, an interesting and potentially concerning situation exists—particularly if leaving is not a viable option. What happens when the two foci come into conflict? Does AC form the basis on which a person will side with one over the other? What are the potential work behavior consequences of this situation? Given that people have commitment to more than one workplace domain, it makes sense to consider how these interact in their impact on work behaviors.

The third issue raised by the CFA results relates to how people come to feel differently about nested foci in the first place. Relatively little work has been done in this area. Thus, although the straightforward answer is simply that AC to A and AC to B (within A) have at least some different antecedents, there has been little empirical demonstration of this with respect to nested collectives. Similarly, the suggestion that the organization and its teams (common examples of nested collectives) often send mixed messages to members, making it difficult for personnel to develop strong commitment to both foci simultaneously (Allen, 1996), has not been tested empirically. Heffner and Gade shed some welcome light on this issue that is consistent with both these general suggestions. They found support for a model, based on Mueller and Lawler's (1999) theorizing about nested collectives, that emphasizes (a) differences in the relative salience of features of foci that are "proximal" (e.g., Special Forces) and "distal" (military) to the individual and (b) the interrelations between satisfaction and commitment to both foci. A greatly simplified summary of their findings suggests that AC to the two foci in question have overlapping, but not identical, predictors—hence their status as related, but discernible, commitments. How can we optimize AC to both (all) nested collectives? Perhaps by insuring that the messages sent by those within each collective are consistent. For example, in addition to providing "positive organizational support" (Eisenberger, Huntington, Hutchison, & Sowa, 1986), ensure that positive support also comes from more proximal sources ("positive team support," "positive supervisory support").

Clearly, there is much to be learned about the multiple foci of work-related commitment. If done in the tradition of a multidimensional view of commitment, this will become very complex. Nonetheless, given the evidence that this approach has added value for predicting work behavior (e.g., Becker & Billings, 1993; Meyer et al., 1993), such research is of considerable importance.

THE MILITARY AS A RESEARCH RESOURCE

The military is an extremely valuable resource both for increasing our understanding of the work attitudes in the military and for the field as a whole. Indeed, the final theme here may best be considered a plea for continued careful management of this valuable resource—there are some golden opportunities here.

Several factors contribute to this. One is the diverse nature of the military workforce itself. In the five studies in this issue, for example, we see wide variation, within and across samples, in terms of demographic variables, jobs, ranks, and respondents' relation to the military (e.g., active, reserve, spouses). Further, some sample sizes in military commitment research (here and elsewhere) rival anything in the commitment literature and would easily allow for the examination of particularly complex issues that have received too little attention (e.g., research on commitment profiles, multiple commitment– multiple foci projects). Another factor lies with personnel practices within the military. To an outsider, at least, there appears to be some tradition of, and mechanisms for, ongoing employee assessment (e.g., attitude surveys, established performance indicators). This is extremely rare within organizational settings and extremely valuable as it represents a critical precondition (a "setting of the stage," so to speak) for meaningful longitudinal examination of many workplace commitment issues. Finally, it is clear that those who are involved in military commitment research are very resourceful and are making effective use of the golden opportunities available to them to achieve both practical and scientific goals.

In my view, there are several directions in which commitment research within the military could proceed. I have touched on most of these throughout my discussion and so mention them only briefly here. First, I think it critical that researchers continue to strive for conceptual and measurement clarity—both for commitment and other variables. Although consistency in how commitment is measured within the military will be useful for benchmarking purposes, it will be important not to settle on a particular set of measures without due consideration to construct validation. Second, and perhaps not surprisingly, I would argue that the potential role of NC needs closer examination within the military than it has been given. Indeed, the military may well be one of the places in which subtler effects of NC on work behavior, particularly highly discretionary behavior, could play themselves out most clearly. Third, and related to this, we need work examining the impact that commitment has on a wider, and richer, set of outcomes. Despite the number of consequence studies in the literature, researchers have only scratched the surface. Little is known, for example, about the relations between commitment and behavior under stressful conditions, teamwork-related behaviors, workplace deviance, or health-related outcomes. Work on the commitment—leadership relation is only just beginning. Commitment has rarely been examined at the group level of analysis where the question is whether aggregated commitment (e.g., across a unit) predicts various aspects of group-level performance (e.g., Allen & Grisaffe, 2001). Ideally, outcomes should be examined as a function of the commitment profile—research that benefits from the large samples available in the military. Fourth, although it is interesting to learn that a particular organizational characteristic, event, or program is related to some component of commitment, both theory building and practice are better served if we determine something about how this occurs. Such knowledge strengthens the nomological network associated with the commitment construct and builds a stronger foundation for managing workplace commitment. Thus we need more fine- grained (and ideally, longitudinal) studies that examine the process through which antecedent variables exert their influence on commitment. In doing so, it will be very important not to overlook the intriguing suggestion made by Tisak and Tisak (2000) and noted by Gade et al. (2003/this issue) that organizational commitment may have "traitlike characteristics" (p. 198). Finally, it will be important to examine each of the antecedent and consequence issues with respect to the interplay between commitment to the organization (military) and other foci. One's commitment to the organization is important, but clearly it will not tell the whole story about the linkages people have with their work.

Many of these issues can be adequately studied only with the involvement of large, relatively stable workforces examined over time. Thus, there is enormous potential within the military. Indeed, given adequate resources, there is every reason to believe that military organizations can continue to play a scientific leadership role in commitment research and, at the same time, provide specific and practical advice to military leaders about the people challenges facing their organization.

REFERENCES

Allen, N. J. (1996). Affective reactions to the group and the organization. In M. A. West (Ed.), *Handbook of work group psychology* (pp. 371–396). Chichester, England: Wiley.

Allen, N. J., & Grisaffe, D. (2001). Employee commitment to the organization and customer reactions: Mapping the linkages. *Human Resource Management Review, 11,* 209–236.

Allen, N. J., & Meyer, J. P. (1990). The measurement and antecedents of affective, continuance, and normative commitment to the organization. *Journal of Occupational Psychology, 63,* 1-18.

Allen, N. J., & Meyer, J. P. (1996). Affective, continuance, and normative commitment to the organization: An examination of construct validity. *Journal of Vocational Behavior, 49,* 252–276.

Allen, N. J., & Meyer, J. P. (2000). Construct validation in organizational behavior: The case of organizational commitment. In R. D. Goffin & E. Helmes (Ed.), *Problems and solutions in human assessment: Honoring Douglas N. Jackson at seventy.* Norwell, MA: Kluwer Academic.

Becker, T. E., & Billings, R. S. (1993). Profiles of commitment: An empirical test. *Journal of Organizational Behavior, 14,* 177–190.

Eisenberger, R., Huntington, R., Hutchison, S., & Sowa, D. (1986). Perceived organizational support. *Journal of Applied Psychology, 71,* 500–507.

Finegan, J. E. (2000). The impact of personal and organizational values on commitment. *Journal of Organizational and Occupational Psychology, 73,* 149–169.

Gade, P.A., Tiggle, R. B., & Schumm, W. R. (2003/this issue). The measurement and consequences of military organizational commitment in soldiers and spouses. *Military Psychology, 15,* 191–207.

Hackett, R. D., Bycio, P., & Hausdorf, P. A. (1994). Further assessments of Meyer and Allen's (1991) three-component model of organizational commitment. *Journal of Applied Psychology, 79,* 15–23.

Heffner, T. S., & Gade, P. A. (2003/this issue). Commitment to nested collectives in Special Operations Forces. *Military Psychology, 15,* 209–223.

Hinkin, T. R. (1995). A review of scale development practices in the study of organizations. *Journal of Management, 21,* 967–988.

Hinkin, T. R. (1998). A brief tutorial in the development of measures for use in survey questionnaires. *Organizational Research Methods, 1,* 104–121.

Hunt, S. D., & Morgan, R. M. (1994). Organizational commitment: One of many commitments or key mediating construct? *Academy of Management Journal, 37,* 1568–1587.

Irving, P. G., Coleman, D. F., & Cooper, C. L. (1997). Further assessments of a three-component model of occupational commitment: Generalizability and differences across occupations. *Journal of Applied Psychology, 82,* 444–452.

Karrasch, A. I. (2003/this issue). Antecedents and consequences of organizational commitment. *Military Psychology, 15,* 225–236.

Koys, D. J. (1991). Fairness, legal compliance, and organizational commitment. *Employee Responsibilities and Rights Journal, 4,* 283–291.

Lee, K., Carswell, J. J., & Allen, N. J. (2000). A meta-analytic review of occupational commitment: Relations with person and work-related variables. *Journal of Applied Psychology, 85,* 799–811.

Mathieu, J. E., & Zajac, D. (1990). A review and meta-analysis of the antecedents, correlates, and consequences of organizational commitment. *Psychological Bulletin, 108,* 171–194.

Mayer, R. C., & Schoorman, F. D. (1992). Predicting participation and production outcomes through a two-dimensional model of organizational commitment. *Academy of Management Journal, 35,* 671–684.

McGee, G. W., & Ford, R. C. (1987). Two (or more?) dimensions of organizational commitment: Re-examination of the Affective and Continuance Commitment Scales. *Journal of Applied Psychology, 72,* 638–642.

Meyer, J. P., & Allen, N. J. (1984). Testing the "side-bet theory" of organizational commitment: Some methodological considerations. *Journal of Applied Psychology, 69,* 372–378.

Meyer, J. P., & Allen, N. J. (1991). A three-component conceptualization of organizational commit-ment. *Human Resource Management Review, 1,* 61–89.

Meyer, J. P., & Allen, N. J. (1997). *Commitment in the workplace: Theory, research and application.* Thousand Oaks, CA: Sage.

Meyer, J. P., Allen, N. J., & Gellatly, I. R. (1990). Affective and continuance commitment to the organi-zation: Evaluation of measures and analysis of concurrent and time-lagged relations. *Journal of Ap-plied Psychology, 75,* 710–720.

Meyer, J. P., Allen, N. J., & Smith, C. A. (1993). Commitment to organizations and occupations: Exten-sion and test of a three-component conceptualization. *Journal of Applied Psychology, 78,* 538–551.

Meyer, J. P., Allen, N. J., & Topolnytsky, L. (1998). Commitment in a changing world of work. *Cana-dian Psychology, 39,* 83–93.

Meyer, J. P., Irving, P. G., & Allen, N. J. (1998). Examination of the combined effects of work values and early work experiences on organizational commitment. *Journal of Organizational Behavior, 19,* 29–52.

Meyer, J. P., Paunonen, S. V., Gellatly, I. H., Goffin, R. D., & Jackson, D. N. (1989). Organizational commitment and job performance: It's the nature of the commitment that counts. *Journal of Applied Psychology, 74,* 152–156.

Meyer, J. P., Stanley, D. J., Herscovitch, L., & Topolnytsky, L. (2002). Affective, continuance, and nor-mative commitment to the organization: A meta-analyses of antecedents, correlates, and conse-quences. *Journal of Vocational Behavior, 61,* 20–52.

Morita, J. G., Lee, T., & Mowday, R. T. (1993). The regression-analog to survivor research: A selected application to turnover research. *Academy of Management Journal, 36,* 1430–1464.

Morrow, P. C. (1993). *The theory and measurement of work commitment.* Greenwich, CT: JAI.

Mowday, R. T., Steers, R. M., & Porter, L. W. (1979). The measurement of organizational commitment. *Journal of Vocational Behavior, 14,* 224–247.

Mueller, C. W., & Lawler, E. J. (1999). Commitment to nested organizational units: Some basic princi-ples and preliminary findings. *Social Psychology Quarterly, 62,* 325–346.

Mueller, C. W., Wallace, J. E., & Price, J. L. (1992). Employee commitment: Resolving some issues. *Work and Occupations, 19,* 211–236.

O'Reilly, C. A., & Chatman, J. (1986). Organizational commitment and psychological attachment: The effects of compliance, identification, and internalization on prosocial behavior. *Journal of Applied Psychology, 71,* 492–499.

Schwab, D. P. (1980). Construct validity in organizational behavior. *Research in Organizational Be-havior, 2,* 3–43.

Sevastos, P., Smith, L., & Cordery, J. L. (1992). Evidence on the reliability and construct validity of Warr's 1990 well-being and mental health measures. *Journal of Occupational and Organizational Psychology, 65,* 33–49.

Somers, M. J. (1993). A test of the relationship between affective and continuance commitment using non-recursive models. *Journal of Occupational and Organizational Psychology, 66,* 185–192.

Tisak, J., & Tisak, M. S. (2000). Permanency and ephemerality of psychological measures with appli-cation to organizational commitment. *Psychological Methods, 5,* 175–198.

Tremble, T. R., Payne, S. C., Finch, J. F., & Bullis, R. C. (2003/this issue). Opening organizational ar-chives to research: Analog measures of organizational commitment. *Military Psychology, 15,* 167–190.

TEAMS THAT LEAD
A Matter of Market Strategy, Leadership Skills, and Executive Strength
Theresa J.B. Kline
University of Calgary

Teams That Lead: A Matter of Market Strategy, Leadership Skills, and Executive Strength strikes a balance between the current scholarly literature that exists in these fields and its impact on teams. The focus on leading executive teams makes this book unique. It provides three lenses with which to view team leadership and how those various lenses can assist in making teams more effective. The first focuses on paying close attention to the market strategy of the organization and how it should drive key decisions. The second focuses on the multiple roles of the designated leader of a team. The third focus shifts to executive teams and how to be a highly effective team player in the executive environment. Each section is grounded in theoretical and empirical evidence. How this information can then be translated into useful knowledge for practitioners and researchers follows. To make it practical, however, the book provides examples, cases, measuring tools, and questions. This book will be of interest to students and professors in MBA programs, organizational behavior, public policy, and psychology courses. Practitioners, such as consultants, facilitators, trainers, and executive coaches will also be interested.

0-8058-4237-3 [cloth] / 2003 / 232pp. / $59.95
0-8058-4542-9 [paper] / 2003 / 232pp. / $24.50
Prices are subject to change without notice.

Lawrence Erlbaum Associates, Inc.
10 Industrial Ave., Mahwah, NJ 07430–2262
201–258–2200; 1–800–926–6579; fax 201–760–3735
orders@erlbaum.com; www.erlbaum.com

SUBSCRIPTION ORDER FORM

Please ❑ enter ❑ renew my subscription to:

MILITARY PSYCHOLOGY

THE OFFICIAL JOURNAL OF THE DIVISION OF MILITARY PSYCHOLOGY
AMERICAN PSYCHOLOGICAL ASSOCIATION, DIVISION 19
Volume 15, 2003, Quarterly — ISSN 0899–5605/Online ISSN 1532–7876

SUBSCRIPTION PRICES PER VOLUME:

Category:	Access Type:	Price: US/All Other Countries
❑ Individual	Online & Print	$60.00/$90.00

Subscriptions are entered on a calendar-year basis only and must be paid in advance in U.S. currency—check, credit card, or money order. Prices for subscriptions include postage and handling. Journal prices expire 12/31/03. **NOTE**: Institutions must pay institutional rates. Individual subscription orders are welcome if prepaid by credit card or personal check. **Please note:** A $20.00 penalty will be charged against customers providing checks that must be returned for payment. This assessment will be made only in instances when problems in collecting funds are directly attributable to customer error.

❑ **Check Enclosed** (U.S. Currency Only)   **Total Amount Enclosed $**_____

❑ **Charge My**: ❑ VISA   ❑ MasterCard   ❑ AMEX   ❑ Discover

Card Number _____   Exp. Date_____/_____

Signature_____
(Credit card orders cannot be processed without your signature.)
PRINT CLEARLY for proper delivery. STREET ADDRESS/SUITE/ROOM # REQUIRED FOR DELIVERY.

Name_____

Address_____

City/State/Zip+4_____

Daytime Phone #_____E-mail address_____
Prices are subject to change without notice.

For information about online subscriptions, visit our website at *www.erlbaum.com*

Mail orders to: **Lawrence Erlbaum Associates, Inc.,** Journal Subscription Department
10 Industrial Avenue, Mahwah, NJ 07430; (201) 258–2200; FAX (201) 760–3735; journals@erlbaum.com

LIBRARY RECOMMENDATION FORM

Detach and forward to your librarian.

❑ I have reviewed the description of *Military Psychology* and would like to recommend it for acquisition.

MILITARY PSYCHOLOGY

THE OFFICIAL JOURNAL OF THE DIVISION OF MILITARY PSYCHOLOGY
AMERICAN PSYCHOLOGICAL ASSOCIATION, DIVISION 19
Volume 15, 2003, Quarterly — ISSN 0899–5605/Online ISSN 1532–7876

Category:	Access Type:	Price: US/All Other Countries
❑ Institutional	Online & Print	$395.00/$425.00
❑ Institutional	Online Only	$355.00/$355.00
❑ Institutional	Print Only	$355.00/$385.00

Name_____Title_____

Institution/Department_____

Address_____

E-mail Address_____
Librarians, please send your orders directly to LEA or contact from your subscription agent.

Lawrence Erlbaum Associates, Inc., Journal Subscription Department
10 Industrial Avenue, Mahwah, NJ 07430; (201) 258–2200; FAX (201) 760–3735; journals@erlbaum.com

EDUCATING THE CONSUMER-CITIZEN

A History of the Marriage of Schools, Advertising, and Media

Joel Spring

New School University

A Volume in the Sociocultureal, Political, and Historical Studies in Education Series

"Joel Spring is the leading historian of education in the United States....This study of the intersection of the rationalization of the labor market (vocational education, tracking, standardized aptitude and intelligence tests); the professionalization and expansion of the advertising industry; the growth of radio, television, and film; and the development of the leisure industry is intellectually provocative and politically urgent."

—**Peter McLaren**
University of California, Los Angeles

In *Educating the Consumer-Citizen: A History of the Marriage of Schools, Advertising, and Media,* Joel Spring charts the rise of consumerism as the dominant American ideology of the 21st century. He documents and analyzes how, from the early 19th century through the present, the combined endeavors of schools, advertising, and media have led to the creation of a consumerist ideology and ensured its central place in American life and global culture.

Spring first defines *consumerist ideology* and *consumer-citizen* and explores their 19th-century origins in schools, children's literature, the commercialization of American cities, advertising, newspapers, and the development of department stores. He then traces the rise of consumerist ideology in the 20th century by looking closely at: the impact of the home economics profession on the education of women as consumers and the development of an American cuisine based on packaged and processed foods; the influence of advertising images of sports heroes, cowboys, and the clean-shaven businessman in shaping male identity; the outcomes of the growth of the high school as a mass institutiton on the development of teenage consumer markets; the consequences of commercial radio and television joining with the schools to educate a consumer-oriented population so that, by the 1950s, consumerist images were tied to the Cold War and presented as the "American way of life" in both media and schools; the effects of the civil rights movement on integrating previously excluded groups into the consumer society; the changes the women's movement demanded in textbooks, school curricula, media, and advertising that led to a new image of women in the consumer market; and the ascent of fast food education. Spring carries the story into the 21st century by examining the evolving marriage of schools, advertising, and media and its ongoing role in educating the consumer-citizen and creating an integrated consumer market.

This book will be of wide interest to scholars, professionals, and students across foundations of education, history and sociology of education, educational policy, mass communications, American history, and cultural studies. It is highly appropriate as a text for courses in these areas.

Contents: Preface. Horace Mann Meets the Wizard of Oz. Liberation With Jell-O and Wonder Bread: Educating the New Woman. Cowboys and Jocks: Visions of Manliness. Commodification of Leisure and Cultural Control: Schools, Movies, and Radio. The American Way and the Manufactuing of Consent. Participating in the American Dream. Sonya's Choice: Fast Food Education.
0-8058-4273-X [cloth] / 2003 / 264pp. / $65.00
0-8058-4274-8 [paper] / 2003 / 264pp. / $24.50
Prices are subject to change without notice.

Lawrence Erlbaum Associates, Inc.
10 Industrial Ave., Mahwah, NJ 07430–2262
201–258–2200; 1–800–926–6579; fax 201–760–3735
orders@erlbaum.com; www.erlbaum.com